GOD'S CHURCH
MY PLACE

Steve Tilley

GOD'S CHURCH MY PLACE

What it means to belong to
a Christian community

Text copyright © Steve Tilley 2012
The author asserts the moral right
to be identified as the author of this work

Published by
The Bible Reading Fellowship
15 The Chambers, Vineyard
Abingdon OX14 3FE
United Kingdom
Tel: +44 (0)1865 319700
Email: enquiries@brf.org.uk
Website: www.brf.org.uk
BRF is a Registered Charity

ISBN 978 0 85746 011 0

First published 2012
10 9 8 7 6 5 4 3 2 1 0
All rights reserved

Acknowledgments
Unless otherwise stated, scripture quotations are taken from the Holy Bible, New International Version, copyright © 1973, 1978, 1984 by International Bible Society, are used by permission of Hodder & Stoughton Publishers, a member of the Hachette Livre Group UK. All rights reserved. 'NIV' is a registered trademark of International Bible Society. UK trademark number 1448790.

Scripture quotations taken from the Holy Bible, Today's New International Version, copyright © 2004 by International Bible Society, are used by permission of Hodder & Stoughton Publishers, a member of the Hachette Livre Group UK. All rights reserved. 'TNIV' is a registered trademark of International Bible Society.

The paper used in the production of this publication was supplied by mills that source their raw materials from sustainably managed forests. Soy-based inks were used in its printing and the laminate film is biodegradable.

A catalogue record for this book is available from the British Library

Printed in Singapore by Craft Print International Ltd

Contents

Introduction 7

1 What is church anyway? 11

2 How to listen to a sermon 22

3 Worship recovery programme 30

4 Intercessions 47

5 Not just me 59

6 The state of the coffee 77

7 Sunday special? 91

8 How to not be a leader 100

9 What is the church doing to my faith? 113

10 Part of the solution or part of the problem? 122

Conclusion 134

Notes 137

Introduction

I have a vision of the best church for miles and miles.

A church where people drop in (parties of 50 or more needing to book) to observe examples of good practice and get a fine cup of free coffee (much improved since Costa got the post-church contract).

A church where the outstanding teaching, heart-lifting worship, dramatic supernatural interventions and free food have made it a place where not to belong to the Jesus-following community is slightly odd.

A church where the outstanding minds from a number of agencies who happen to live here get together over a drink regularly and put the world to rights, not just with words but with reality. Their conversation becomes action; fewer people are poor around the world because of the influence of this brainstorming community.

A church where the recent outpouring of generosity led to twice as much money as was necessary being promised towards the new building project, as a result of which two new churches were also built on less fortunate estates.

A church that provides the finances to improve local surgeries, attract new businesses to town and sponsor a football team now rising rapidly towards the higher leagues.

A church whose potential ministers are wooed by theological colleges, whose staff-in-training are expected to take substantial responsibility as soon as they move on and whose missionaries only have to set foot elsewhere to start major outpourings of grace and mercy.

I know, I know. Carlsberg (probably) don't do churches. But if they did…

If they did, they would be churches that were about the members, not the leaders.

What is this book *not* going to be about? Leadership, that's what. In fact, the aim will be to avoid all the suggestions included in the following comment, which I received when I asked around to see what people thought the book should cover:

I'm intrigued that, having been a leader in Christian ministry for over 25 years, you wish to write a book on 'what it is like to be led'. I've no doubt you would have many insightful comments born out of a wide range of experience:
Ten things not to say to your leader.
Joys and frustrations of parish life.
Great things about my job.
How to avoid being a heart-sink parishioner.
What I would like you to be like if I was leading you.

It was helpful to read this observation. It would be so easy to fall into the trap of writing from the frustrations of being a leader, but I will try not to. The comment was anonymous: I fear the commenter belongs to my church.

I have sat in meetings where two people were trying to lead at the same time. Truth be told, the rest of us may as well have worn helmets while the pair of them sorted out who was in charge. Two leaders in a meeting is one too many. Local churches can have different people heading up ministries but only one overall leader—which means that everyone else is a follower.

Can you recall ever reading a book on how to be a follower?

My wife works as an area manager in retail. One of the ways her company assesses its work is to send round mystery shoppers with hidden cameras. The DVDs of the 'performance' are then sent to the management team to critique. I have sat on the sofa next to her on many evenings as she has screamed at the screen in anguish at a lowly shop assistant's failure to do the right thing—or observed her glowing sense of pride when someone did a great job. Those mystery shoppers are primed to ask very awkward questions.

OK, so it's tough being the boss. But we don't live in a world of bosses (thankfully). What should our attitude be if we are employees trying to please the boss, or trying to work round her?

Can you recall ever reading a book about how to get things done when you're not the boss?

This is a question for the church, too, because when the mystery worshippers come round (and be sure, such people do exist and their reports can be read), it is not only the boss's job to make sure they have a good experience but the employees' job too. Not just the minister's but the members'.

That is why I've written this book. What are the tricks of the trade in being a church member? How do you—as a member, not a leader—make sure any visitor to your church meeting, any newcomer to your local community, any enquirer into faith, gets the best possible experience of local Christianity?

Can you recall reading a book reminding leaders that they have nothing to do if there's no one to lead?

Actually, if you've read the letter to the Ephesian Christians in the Bible, you may have done:

[God's] intent was that now, through the church, the manifold wisdom of God should be made known to the rulers and authorities in the heavenly realms, according to his eternal purpose that he accomplished in Christ Jesus our Lord. (Ephesians 3:10–11)

Did you see that? 'Through the church', not 'through the leader of the church'.

Ephesians is going to figure heavily in our journey. You might like to read it first, but don't worry if you want to dive straight into this book. I'll try to keep you up to speed.

In all the many words written about belonging to a church, there is often an overemphasis on leadership. What about membership? What is required of someone who simply wants to learn what it means to be part of a church without any aspirations of leadership? If that's you, welcome aboard my hobby-horse. The metaphors may get a bit mixed but there's no need to strap yourself in. We will go slowly and tread carefully.

What is church anyway?

'And I tell you that you are Peter, and on this rock I will build my church…'
MATTHEW 16:18

The problem with Christianity in this country is that there are too many churches; the Gospel paradox is that the solution is to build more.
STEPHEN COTTRELL, BISHOP OF CHELMSFORD[1]

Jesus changed the apostle Simon's name to Peter, which comes from the Greek word *petros*, meaning 'rock'. Matthew 16:18 contains the first reference to church in the Bible. In my Bible, church is not mentioned until page 1146. The word 'church' is not in any Gospel other than Matthew's.

Peter had just tumbled on to an important truth about Jesus. He had said, 'You are the Christ, the Son of the living God' (v. 16).

Peter had got it. Church is a collection of people who have got it. Not musicianship. Not preaching skills. Certainly not buildings. Not dress codes. Not Sunday ritual. Just truth—the truth about Jesus. That is the rock.

After Jesus' death and resurrection, the agreed word for a gathering of Christians soon became 'church': 'Great fear seized the whole church and all who heard about these events' (Acts 5:11). 'I commend to you our sister Phoebe, a servant of the church in Cenchrea… Greet Priscilla and

Aquila… Greet also the church that meets at their house' (Romans 16:1, 3, 5).

Thereafter, many of the letters in the New Testament are addressed to churches: 'To the church of God in Corinth…' (1 Corinthians 1:2). 'To the church of the Thessalonians…' (1 Thessalonians 1:1). 'To Philemon our dear friend and fellow worker, to Apphia our sister, to Archippus our fellow soldier and to the church that meets in your home…' (Philemon 1–2).

Or they deal with specific problems in churches: 'Try to excel in gifts that build up the church' (1 Corinthians 14:12b). 'If anyone does not know how to manage his own family, how can he take care of God's church?' (1 Timothy 3:5). 'Is any one of you sick? He should call the elders of the church to pray over him' (James 5:14).

Soon after Peter got it, churches had appeared and started to have problems. If they hadn't had any difficulties, the New Testament may well have stopped at the book of Acts.

But Peter had got it. And the problem with that? There are many, but one is that we built buildings on real rock, not churches on the metaphor.

Bishop Stephen Cottrell was saying that many of our church buildings are in the wrong place. (Don't worry about what I was doing at a National Stewardship Advisers' Conference. It's a long story and really quite dull.)

I belong to the Church of England, a church which has left the evidence of its past scattered across the landscape of England, sometimes marking the way but often out of the way. Our buildings are, in many cases, in the wrong place but we have a duty to care for them.

Costs of repairs to ancient and heritage-rich church buildings are largely borne by the congregations who happen to meet there. Often, funds that could be better spent on talking of Jesus are used on repairs. Congregations that could leave their church buildings to fall into disrepair while meeting somewhere else usually choose not to—which is good of them. On one level, this impresses people. On another it is a real barrier to mission.

We do well to remind ourselves that Christianity has a nomadic heritage. God does not live in a building—any building. 'The God who made the world and everything in it is the Lord of heaven and earth and does not live in temples built by hands' (Acts 17:24).

Note the language of my Licence (the permission I have to work in a particular place as a priest):

WE do hereby grant you our Licence and authority to serve during our pleasure at a Stipend in accordance with the Diocesan scale for an incumbent as Assistant Curate (having the status and title of Associate Vicar) of the Benefice of Nailsea Holy Trinity within our Diocese and Jurisdiction under the direction of the Reverend Kenneth John Boullier the Incumbent thereof and to perform all ecclesiastical duties belonging to that office with special responsibilities for the Trendlewood area AND ALSO Licence and Authority (so long as you are licensed to the said benefice) to minister in the Benefices of Nailsea Christ Church with Tickenham and Wraxall with Failand within our Diocese and Jurisdiction to perform ecclesiastical duties in these benefices in co-operation with the Ministers in charge thereof…

Below this is the seal of the Bishop of Bath and Wells.

We have buildings in the wrong place and words that no

one else uses. Yet churches are full of people fascinated by and in love with Jesus, seeking after the truth of what that means, still trying to care for and live with those who come to different conclusions, and feeling that there is as much wisdom in the journey as the destination.

The church I minister at is changing venue. We have no building of our own and have just stopped meeting in one local school to move to another. I am writing this before our first meeting in our new place. This week we are homeless. It is good to remind ourselves from time to time, as a Christian community, that we are on the move, responding to God's call not to stay put but to go:

'You will be my witnesses in Jerusalem, and in all Judea and Samaria, and to the ends of the earth.' (Acts 1:8)

When the New Testament was written down, it is likely that my current home was either under water or, at best, a tidal island. You can't get much more ends-of-the-earth than that. It wasn't even earth. The gospel reached Nailsea because faithful followers of the one who used to be dead brought it here. I think they might have been surprised at how quickly it settled down, built itself a home and put its feet up.

I'll let you know later in the book what happened at our first meeting of Trendlewood Church in Golden Valley school. At the moment, I'm in that zombie world between terrified and excited.

Buildings can confuse the call to be church. Being church means being ready to go.

Recently I had to tell a 9.00am congregation that someone had died. Since the person had died overnight, it was information that hadn't yet filtered through to most of those present. There was a bit of a gasp and some corporate shock.

It took me back to Wishaw, a little country parish in the Midlands, where I found myself officiating at an early Communion on the Sunday when Princess Diana had died (in the early hours of that morning, you may recall). Those who had come to church without switching on a radio or TV first were completely shaken.

But it also does us good to remember times before TV, radio, the internet and telephone—the times when most of our church buildings were constructed. I imagine that much news of the local community was passed on when people gathered, and they gathered at the church. News of recent deaths would have been the minister's task to communicate, and this in an age when the infant mortality rate was much higher than it is now.

Church is about gathered people. So it is about being ready to go and being prepared to stay and minister among a particular community.

Should I stay or should I go? Can't this God make his flipping mind up? As with much of our Bible, there are complementary truths to consider.

Those of us who have been part of the same Christian community in the same place for a long time need to remind ourselves that God calls people out and on. Those of us who have been on the move a lot need to heed the call to stay put and be part of the church planted in a particular place. Both groups of people should take time out to call to mind what it is like to be in the other group.

Church is about gathered people, and many of those gatherings take place in buildings that were designed for a different sort of life. In some of them you can also tell, from the size of the pews, that people used to be shorter.

Over the next couple of decades, what it means to be church is going to change dramatically. As it does, the best versions (franchises if you like) of the old way of doing church will thrive. Brian McLaren tells a story, in his book *A New Kind of Christian*, about transport. A character in the book asks, 'If you were going to buy the best possible mode of transport in 1910, what would you buy?'[2]

To paraphrase the answer, many would say that the age of the car was just beginning and they would buy a car. They'd be wrong. As the age of the car was just beginning, cars were incredibly unreliable and dangerous. If you wanted reliability you'd buy a buggy. Buggy technology had reached a pinnacle and only the very best buggy manufacturers remained in business. Horses were reliable.

As churches die out all over the place, they are like buggy manufacturers going out of business. Anyone wanting a church will go to a surviving one. The remaining ones will get bigger and better. There will be more and more attendees at fewer and fewer churches.

Have you seen the car coming? Many haven't. Meanwhile, buggy manufacturing churches will fall away because of:

- Buildings being in the wrong place.
- A treatment of women in leadership, or the gay and lesbian community, that our society and culture will not accept.
- Failure to attract younger members.
- Better and bigger churches being more attractive.

- Insistence on newcomers eventually ticking boxes to do with minor bits of doctrine.
- Failure to ditch the 'Bible as history' model and to embrace science.

And then the car will come…

I'm sure, from then on, the buggy preservation society will exist and will have an enthusiastic and active membership who get together, show off their polished buggies and talk about the old days. But everyone else will have moved on and, if truth be told, will have ceased being very interested in buggies. I wonder what the *car* church will look like.

Let's see if we can do the world's briefest history of the modern church.

After Jesus' ministry, there was a group of followers. Soon they split into those who remained Jews and part of Judaism, and those who didn't. Christianity survived in those who didn't. Three centuries later, this one worldwide (therefore, catholic with a small 'c', from a Greek word meaning 'universal') church had a dispute over a couple of small but important words, and the Eastern Orthodox Church and the Roman Church separated.

A thousand years or so passed until King Henry VIII of England required an annulment of his first marriage. When the Pope refused, Henry appointed himself Supreme Head of the English Church in 1534. This act is often seen as the key moment in a long process by which the church in England became reformed, but of course the Reformation (rediscovery of biblical truth and God's grace) had begun in Europe and continued after Henry's reign. Luther, Calvin and the like did their best work in the late 15th and early 16th centuries.

A person who accepts the system of faith and practice of the reformed church is a Protestant, from the Latin *protestari*, which means 'to witness before'.

There are many reforming processes going on in Roman Catholicism and Protestantism today and, of course, there are also those who are part of the Church of England yet consider themselves Catholic. Down the ages, the terms have become symptomatic of community division. The troubles and struggles in Northern Ireland got short-handed as Catholic v. Protestant, but they were always about nationality and government, not religion. Hence the joke:

'Are you a Catholic or a Protestant?'
'I'm an atheist.'
'Yes, but are you a Catholic atheist or a Protestant one?'

Methodism has its roots in John Wesley's revival movement, set within Anglicanism. The Methodist Church did not become separate until after his death. Methodism and Anglicanism continue to take tentative steps towards agreement and merger.

In February 2010, the then Methodist President David Gamble, addressing the General Synod of the Church of England, said this:

Methodists approach the Covenant with the Church of England in the spirituality of the Covenant prayer, so when we say to God, 'Let me have all things, let me have nothing', we say it by extension to our partners in the Church of England as well. We are prepared to go out of existence not because we are declining or failing in mission, but for the sake of mission. In other words, we are prepared to be changed and even to cease having a separate existence as a Church if that will serve the needs of the kingdom.

It remains one of the most gloriously open, vulnerable, humble and risky statements I have ever heard from a church leader. Maximum respect.

Baptists trace their history to the early part of the 17th century. The roots of the movement are the belief that a correct reading of the New Testament is to practise only believer's baptism, not infant baptism, and to do so by immersion.

In recent times, the house church movement, free evangelicalism, Pentecostalism, Vineyard churches and a succession of movements within mainstream denominations have been typified by a lively style of sung worship and the use of spiritual gifts and prayer ministry. Most practise believer's, not infant, baptism.

There is a wonderful timeline of the key events in Christianity at en.wikipedia.org/wiki/Timeline_of_Christianity.

A slightly cynical friend of mine once said that when two churches merge, a third is usually formed.

Some churches these days are quite eclectic. That is a technical word but it means 'gathered'. Those who prefer that church's style, theology or even building may travel quite a way to be part of it. Other churches are local. They minster to a particular area and do not seek to evangelise beyond some specific boundaries.

My own Church of England is local. I minister in a particular part of a particular parish. We get on well with our neighbours but we don't, for instance, drop leaflets through the doors of those who live outside our parish boundary.

What makes a church a church and not a cult? Belief in the Lordship of Christ and some understanding of the Trinity usually mark out a denomination of the mainstream church from a cult. Other differences of belief are usually the wrapping paper, not the parcel.

'I'm such a bad scholar, I feel like a man with a white cane bumping into knowledge.'
THE NARRATOR IN *ILLYWHACKER* BY PETER CAREY[3]

History lesson over. Told you it would be quick.

You might want to read the last few paragraphs again. If you are an academic theologian of church history, don't write in unless I've goofed big-time. This summary has been hopelessly inadequate, possibly to the point of offence, but it is part of a short book.

Many fine works have been written, putting flesh on these bones. The important truth is that the church is there to create the space in which people can find that they have been found by God.

Today, the place of Jesus is 'the church, which is his body, the fullness of him who fills everything in every way' (Ephesians 1:22–23). The Bible suggests that if you want to know what God looks like, you should look at Jesus, the image of the invisible God. And if you want to know what Jesus looks like, you should be able to find out by looking at the church.

Now, is our church worth looking at? If people look, will they see Jesus?

Can you be a Christian without going to church? Possibly, but you are depriving a group of Christians of your gifts and input. I don't think you can be a Christian without somehow being church. You need to work out how you are going to be accountable. This is not a leadership/control thing. We are all perfectly capable of making ourselves accountable to each other. But we need to give someone permission to ask us how we are doing in our prayer life, worship life and service life. The New Testament knows nothing of a Christian outside a community of other believers.

Pause for thought

Church is something that you are rather than somewhere that you go.

Discussion questions

- In what groups of people, then, are you church?
- What is your personal denominational history?
- How many generations of your family have been Christians?

Prayer

Lord, help me to understand what it is to be part of the church.

— ❖ —

How to listen to a sermon

'Great is the Lord's anger that burns against us because our fathers have not obeyed the words of this book; they have not acted in accordance with all that is written there concerning us.'
2 KINGS 22:13B

Our curse as humans is that we are trapped in time; our curse is that we are forced to interpret life as a sequence of events—a story—and when we can't figure out what our particular story is, we feel lost somehow.
KAREN, IN *PLAYER ONE* BY DOUGLAS COUPLAND [4]

Many of Coupland's characters are lost, trapped in contemporary culture. They seek wisdom but have no idea who to listen to.

The Old Testament is tremendously enthusiastic about obedience. How did the people know if they had been obedient? Easy. Things went well—prosperity, victory in battle, good harvests, that sort of thing.

And disobedience? It tended, in their view, to have the opposite results. Famine, poverty, illness and defeat were the four horsemen of naughtiness. If things went badly, people reckoned they must have disobeyed God.

It was a very, ahem, Old Testament way of seeing the world. We have grown up a bit since King Josiah's staff found a bit of Deuteronomy in a cupboard and a whole load of garment-rending followed.

Today we understand obedience to God in a far more individual way. We tend to ask, 'What does God want of me?' rather than, 'What does God want of us?' And we rip our clothes a little less.

What might it mean for a group of Christians in a particular place in the early part of the third millennium ad to work out how to be obedient to God? The minister might say, 'God is calling us to do this.' How do you test that call?

Or the church might have a more corporate leadership. They might all declare, 'We should plant this church… buy this building… give half our money away to Africa.' How do you, an ordinary member of the church, know if what they are calling you to do is what God is calling you to do?

By and large, you don't.

The starting point, it seems to me, is to be in the habit of listening and to be in the habit of testing what you listen to.

Testing? Yes, testing—testing against the one way in which God has spoken to his people, irrevocably, firmly and once-and-for-all. Through Jesus.

How do we know what he has said through Jesus? Through scripture. And how do we learn to listen to the voice of God speaking about Jesus through scripture once-and-for-all?

Then Peter stood up with the Eleven, raised his voice and addressed the crowd: 'Fellow Jews and all of you who live in Jerusalem, let me explain this to you; listen carefully to what I say…' (Acts 2:14)

We learn by listening to sermons. They're that important.

The early evangelical Christians were known as 'enthusiasts'. It was an insult at the time. On the wall of a church in Berkshire there used to be a plaque to a previous minister who preached there for many years 'without enthusiasm'. His parishioners were, apparently, grateful.

But for most people who are not called to preach, enthusiastically or otherwise, are there techniques to be used, to enable feeding on God's word to happen?

It is my firm view that I am a very poor preacher. I have done it a couple of thousand times, though, and I am beginning to get the hang of it. I am trying to improve. It is also possible—because in this country the standard seems to be low—that I am above average.

One of the obstacles I have begun to get over is the idea that preaching is a one-way process. All I am trying to do when I preach is to start a discussion—a discussion in which I might be wrong.

How do you listen to a sermon? Ideally, you'd do it interactively. So you'd say, at the point at which the thought occurs to you, 'I wonder if you could expand on that a bit' or 'Is it possible that this other way of seeing that is helpful?' or 'Rubbish', if you must. The bigger the crowd, the harder that is to do.

What sort of preacher would be comfortable with that level of interruption? A good one. At the minimum, our preachers would become thicker-skinned. But if your minister is not ready for that yet, I am sure she would be still delighted to hear what you made of what she said. What did you do in the light of her teaching? Tell her. How did you get on with the recommended spiritual exercise for the week?

Let's eavesdrop on a great piece of sermon teaching. Paul is in Athens, in the market place. He is hanging about in the place where people hang about, and speaking to people who like talking about the latest ideas (Acts 17:21).

He tells them about Jesus. Well, we think to ourselves, Paul was a great man, a great convert and a great speaker. He was bound to have success. Did he?

Some of them sneered, but others said, 'We want to hear you again...' A few... became followers. (vv. 32, 34)

Three sorts of reaction—sneering, questioning, following.

It was one of the greatest sermons of all time and perhaps the first example of cross-cultural evangelism, but it did not lead to repentance in the streets. It led to some sneering, a bit of 'Tell us more' and a few converts. But it started a conversation.

I almost always take notes on sermons. Sometimes this is because I have been specifically asked to give feedback to preachers I am trying to train. On other occasions it is to help me listen. I like to mull things over and think things through, but also, if left to listen in my own way, I can get sidetracked. My butterfly brain will be attracted to one thought or idea and will pursue it.

Note-taking keeps me on track. Taking notes is not an admission of inability; nor is it a sign of being teacher's pet. These days you don't even need pen and paper, since you probably carry a mobile device with you that has the ability to act as a notepad.

If all else fails and the sermon is deadly dull or inaccurate, try to muse on the Bible passage or text being considered. What would you want to explain? What is the key point?

What is the subtext? What is the backstory? What does this passage say uniquely? What seems odd to you? Maybe you could then send your unanswered questions to the preacher. Good or bad, there is always something to learn.

To get back to the point, why is listening to the sermon part of learning to be in a church community that is obedient to God?

Firstly because, as someone commented on my blog once, 'Education has changed from teaching facts to teaching people how to learn. One of the most important skills now is being able to learn new things.'[5]

So listening to someone talking is a way to relate to the subject matter. Exercising discernment about how convincing the speaker is being is a skill now familiar to many.

Secondly, because if the sermon is challenging the church to move in a particular direction or do a particular thing, you will be able to get on board. As you listen, you will not find yourself saying 'Yes, but…' You will be saying, 'Yes, and…' You will be improving the idea, moving it on, making it apply in a particular place.

I recall hearing someone say, 'In churches there is not a culture of being critical about things you are enjoying.' Being a critical listener is about tweaking, applying, extending and moulding. That is your job as you listen to your leaders. Listening to a sermon will be good practice for listening to all sorts of communication. If you already shout at the TV or radio when you disagree, you are well on the way.

As you learn to listen, you will find yourself getting used to apologetics and doctrine. Themes will recur. Different preachers will have a different take on similar themes. By listening to others, you will find your own view appearing—

in the same way that you decide how to vote, all being well, by listening to the contrasting arguments of the candidates.

I mentioned a spiritual exercise for the week. When I preach, I try to set people one. If the preacher doesn't set me one, I try to invent one. What one thing, I ask myself, do I want to try to do this week as a result of listening to this sermon?

Another great thing to do is to be part of a small group that regularly feeds on God's word. This would be a great place to introduce outstanding questions about last week's sermon.

A word or two about those Christian communities in which every presentation is followed by a time of what they call 'ministry'. Several words, in fact. *It is not compulsory.*

You can enjoy the sung worship and pick the bits out of the talks and presentations without having to subscribe to the view that the *only* way to respond to God is to go down the front and get ministered to by someone who will pray for you to have more Holy Spirit. Often, at festivals and such gatherings, I tend to pray quietly for a few moments and then slink off. I like to reflect. For me, there are several ways to respond to a sermon. Being prayed for is one of them, but only one.

I love the Bible and I do treat it as authoritative. I can make the statement, 'The Bible is true', but that won't help others to work out what I mean and what sort of 'true' it is. I can make the statement, 'I believe in God the Father Almighty', but frankly there is a lot of metaphor packed in there, so it needs investigating before I can know if I am in broad agreement with others who say the same thing.

At a recent Church Council meeting, where we had agreed that the Bible had different things to say on the subject of divorce, without complete consistency, one person put a hand on the Bible at the end of the meeting and said (I can't recall the exact words, so the quote marks are a little unfair), 'I stand by what's in this book.' That disappointed me immensely. It was said as if it solved the problem, whereas that was the problem—the one we had been discussing for the previous hour.

I think I like the self-delineation 'liberal' in the same way that some black people like the N word. I want to rescue it from being a term of abuse to being a matter of pride. I'm liberal. I think for myself. I help others to think. I try to see things from both sides. I'm a Bible-believing liberal. I'm a Jesus-centred liberal. It does make listening a bit easier if you haven't decided whether the speaker is right or wrong before you've heard them.

I understand that faithful, thinking, Bible-believing Christians disagree about divorce, homosexual behaviour, baptism rites, prophecy, women in leadership, eucharistic practice and interfaith dialogue, to name but a few. And I believe that the conversation and the way it is conducted are as important as the outcome.

Because, from the beginning, God said, 'I'm gonna put this world into your hands. If I run everything, then that's not you.' So we were created with a piece of divinity inside us, but with this thing called free will, and I think God watches us every day, lovingly, praying we will make the right choices.
THE REB, IN *HAVE A LITTLE FAITH* BY MITCH ALBON [6]

I like the emotion in this quotation, although I wonder who Mitch thinks God prays to. Maybe he imagines God's hopes for us as prayers because, when God thinks, it must be a prayer—as that is a 'holy' word. I don't know the mind of Mitch Albon, let alone the mind of God.

I do know that at the end of the book of Job, when God finally responds, he speaks in questions, not statements. He asks so many questions that Job's answer, having listened to God, is, 'Surely I spoke of things I did not understand, things too wonderful for me to know' (42:3b).

I'm not the church. We are. So could you listen to me with that in mind, please? Thank you.

Pause for thought

Listen now and let God speak.

Discussion questions

- **Have you had good or bad experiences of listening to sermons?**
- **List the five sermons that have most influenced you.**
- **Now list the five Christians who have most influenced you.**
- **Which list was easier to make, and why?**

Prayer

Lord, help me to listen.

3

Worship recovery programme

When he opened the seventh seal, there was silence in heaven for about half an hour.
REVELATION 8:1

We never needed a self-appointed quango of jaded vampires to tell us how to sing the blues... we got Mojo. We have the power to raise the dead.
ALABAMA 3 [7]

'My friend visited a church in the slums of Nairobi. The Sunday morning service begins at...'

Now, this sentence has a catch in it, caused by our Developed World preoccupation with getting to places on time. The Nairobi service starts when someone gets there. That person potters around sorting a few things out until a second person arrives. Then they sing as they set up. When most people are there, the singing is pretty loud and rather good. So a few sermons and notices and some prayers take place, and people start drifting off to prepare food while those remaining sing a bit more, until the last few tidy up a bit, singing the while. It can take four hours and, if you are a visiting Christian, you'd better be ready to preach for 20 minutes on any subject.

'Silence in heaven for half an hour.' As I heard Gerald Coates say at a worship seminar once, 'Make the most of it, folks; it's all you're getting.'

I visited a cathedral church in the Midlands. I wondered why there was so little opportunity to join in with the worship. There were so many choral items. The Dean said, 'Ah well, you have to get used to worshipping with your ears.'

Maybe, somewhere in between these two extremes, sits the church you belong to and its weekly meeting.

At one act of alternative worship I was involved in, we invited everyone to bring along an everyday object that was mainly red. As a symbol of the offering of our everyday lives to God, we began our time by making a shrine of these red things at the front of our church. We then followed through the theme of 'red' in the Bible, seeing our sins as scarlet and reading about the blood of sacrifices, ending with the sharing of a cup of wine. The preacher used only questions. There were no answers. There was ambient instrumental music all the time, but no singing. We knew what some of it meant but parts of it simply felt right.

In a little country church, five of us huddled around a portable heater in the chancel as we said Evening Prayer, using psalms and readings to lead us to pray for our community. There was no music, no refreshment, and we all hurried off at the end because there were no toilets either.

Maybe, somewhere in between these two extremes, sits the church you belong to and its weekly meeting.

In the back row of the evening service, young people are playing 'spot the tune' as the songs and hymns are sung. They think they have found that 'Lord I lift your name on high' is 'Wild thing', 'Blessed be your name' is 'Let it be', and 'Give thanks with a grateful heart' is 'Go west'. Bored with this game, they move on to the 'Countdown' hymn board challenge, where the bottom number of the four needs to be calculated using all the digits of the previous three hymn numbers. During the sermon, they watch the vicar for any cricket umpire signals and score accordingly.

Elsewhere, prior to the induction of the new vicar, the organist plays the sort of music that leaves you with the vague feeling that you're in some ante-room of hell. You expect 'The Prince of Darkness will see you now' to come booming out over the PA system. Not that the PA system challenges adequacy to any sort of competition. Even the stone-coloured speakers cling, chameleon-esque, to the pillars as if they hope not to be recognised in such a place. The look on the face of the new minister as the solo chorister sings will live with you for a while.

Maybe, somewhere in between these two extremes, sits the church you belong to and its weekly meeting.

Radio 4's Sunday morning service comes on just after 8.00 am. While sorting out washing and unloading dishwashers that have been working their technological magic on your dirt during the night, you turn on the radio. Then, from a small, previously unheard-of Presbyterian community comes an act of worship with sing-songy ministers' voices, a bit of chanting and an overwhelming theme of, well, worthiness.

In a big top, a band in the indie-rock tradition leads singing very loudly. There are guitar, bass, drums, keys, vocals and a backing singer. After 30 minutes or so there is a prayer, and then the speaker comes on, gingering the large crowd up for an hour or so before everyone who wants to respond is implored to come to the front where someone will pray for them.

Maybe, somewhere in between these two extremes, sits the church you belong to and its weekly meeting.

You see, we have a problem with what we do when we meet on a Sunday. We are all different and we don't all like the same stuff. If a church service came along that was utterly 'you' and ticked every one of your worship requirement boxes, there would be only one problem: you'd be alone. And who would operate the smoke machine then?

Here's a real moment from a real church a few years back. It was Pentecost morning, time for the Christian celebration of the coming of the Holy Spirit. Everyone, ironically, behaved as if they had been at an all-night party. Song words were projected in the wrong order. Musicians started the wrong song in the wrong key at the wrong speed (otherwise, fine). The organist arrived after the service had begun. The PA was not turned up until halfway through the service leader's first sentence. The service leader then got a nose bleed. Said two newcomers afterwards, 'We love this church; the welcome is lovely and nobody minds if anyone makes a mistake.'

Within church communities all round the country—indeed, world—there is a battle going on between what individuals want and what everybody wants. At its best, we end up finding parts of an act of worship with which we totally identify, or occasional acts of worship that completely bless us and others that leave us cold. At its worst, like a jam stain on a wedding dress, we only notice the bad bit, even though the rest might be pristine and immaculate.

Let's turn to scripture. It's been too long.

The Old Testament is the story of a people becoming a worshipping community. A proliferation of gods and idols settles down into what we call monotheism—worshipping the one true God. On the journey, stones are raised to mark places where God appeared: 'Jacob... thought, "Surely the Lord is in this place and I was not aware of it." ... Jacob took the stone... and set it up as a pillar' (Genesis 28:17–18).

Altars are set up 'to be a witness... that we will worship the Lord at his sanctuary' (Joshua 22:27).

A tabernacle is erected to house the holy book: 'Make the tabernacle with ten curtains of finely twisted linen and blue, purple and scarlet yarn, with cherubim worked into them by a skilled craftsman' (Exodus 26:1).

Eventually a temple is built: 'In the four hundred and eightieth year after the Israelites had come out of Egypt, in the fourth year of Solomon's reign over Israel, in the month of Ziv, the second month, he began to build the temple of the Lord' (1 Kings 6:1).

Each successive structure is more ornate than the previous one and each is built by skilled craftspeople filled with the Holy Spirit. There is a sense of a people beginning to learn to offer their best to God.

By the time of the social reformer prophets Amos and Hosea, though, people can't wait to get out of worship so that they can get back to exploiting the poor: '"When will the New Moon be over that we may sell grain, and the Sabbath be ended that we may market wheat?"—skimping the measure, boosting the price and cheating with dishonest scales, buying the poor with silver' (Amos 8:5–6).

You get the picture. Amos was not a happy bunny. Temples, shrines and holy places are a fat lot of good if they make no difference to your behaviour once you've worshipped there. Worship is about your behaviour seven days a week, as well as what you do in church.

In his commentary, Alec Motyer paraphrases Philippians 1:27—2:1 as follows:

I have a single desire that your daily life should match the worth of the gospel. Without such a life you will never hold your ground against the world, strong in what God has done for you, unanimous, jointly working for your common faith. But such steadfastness has great results: it convicts the world and convinces you; it condemns the world; it confirms the church. Therefore make my joy full by being of the same mind.[8]

'Being of the same mind'—the same mind as Jesus had, and the same mind on Monday as you have on Sunday.

Jesus was just as scathing as Amos. Sabbaths had, by his day, become so regulation-ridden that the law-makers had a long list of what you could and could not do on that day. Jesus healed someone on the sabbath and was told off for it: 'The synagogue ruler said to the people, "There are six days for work. So come and be healed on those days, not on the Sabbath"' (Luke 13:14).

How mixed up had religious life become, that demonstrating the healing mercy of God was seen as work? Missed the point? They wouldn't have recognised the point if they'd been stabbed with it.

The point of gathering to worship is to equip us to be God's people the rest of the week. If it is not doing that for you, see if you can figure out what needs to change and who you can talk to. Even today, churches get a bit stuck in ruts, slowed down by tradition and unable to move.

So?

What do you think of music? At a Deanery Synod (I'll explain later) meeting recently, a guest spoke to us on church music. For 45 minutes he sang to us, taught us, encouraged us to look welcoming as we sang words of welcome and happy when we sang words of praise, and cheered most people up with his dizzy enthusiasm for the sort of light choral tosh that floats the boat of 75 per cent of Anglicans. 'Mate, it's no good telling people to smile as they sing if, ten minutes earlier, you scowled when you asked them to "move the piano",' I thought, but managed not to say it.

Our Area Dean posed a question: 'Which radio station do you listen to, and how are you taking into account the needs and preferences of those who are different?' The choices in this quiz were:

- Radio 1
- Radio 2
- Radio 3
- Radio 4

Since the answer for me, from these four choices, is Radio 4, but never for music apart from 'Desert Island Discs', I felt it was a bit rich. What of us 6music lovers? Or Rinse FM? Or Spotify? Do people know these stations exist? Someone even heckled, 'What about Classic FM?' I agree. What about Classic FM?

During the course of this evening, someone said, 'Everyone likes singing.'

No they don't. Amazingly, some don't. Twelve-year-old boys whose voices are breaking can find it a nightmare. Some people simply don't approach life musically at all. Often, on bereavement visits, I look around to see if there is any music reproduction equipment on view. Regularly enough, there isn't.

My colleagues in the local Baptist Church now have a music-free Sunday evening service. It simply consists of, I believe, an opening prayer, a Bible exposition and study time in groups. What is church for people who don't like music or don't want to sing? It is a serious question.

That said, anybody leaving a church because they don't like the style of musical worship has just not got a grip on what it means to be a Christian. I met such a person the other day, but I didn't tackle him on his views as he raised them during a compassionate visit. This is so often the case, and it's frustrating. If people in the depths of grief or illness say stupid things, you just have to listen, not challenge. Putting a date in the diary for a row in six months' time is rarely an edifying thing to do. You have to let it lie.

The person concerned left his church's morning service when they introduced new, modern songs. He started attending in the evening, but then they introduced the new songs in the evening service, too, so he stopped attending that. The church in question rarely sings anything less than 20 years old. It is a slow changer, for sure.

The same person also had a go at me because one of the church buildings in our Local Ministry Group has been reordered and chairs put in. Actually, that reordering involved removing a couple of *new* bits of the building's history—a gallery and pews. The reordering has restored it to its original 15th-century style, to a large extent. I did point this out, but felt that I had crossed a line of some sort and was becoming vulnerable to the accusation of arguing at an inappropriate time. I prayed and left.

So what does your perfect church look like? And if you join it, would it still look the same? I don't think I know anybody (Google and let me know) who would find themselves drawn into worship by the improvised Scandinavian musicians Jaga Jazzist, but I would. If I found a church full of people who were captivated and wanting to pray because of their music, I would want to join. I wouldn't play it to any of my current congregations because I know it would be divisive—divisive in the sense that everyone else would hate it.

Lowest common denominator music has been the bane of lower church life. We simply don't have the talent of cathedral choirs, or large congregations full of members of the music industry. On the odd occasions when I have felt that I broke out and tried something different, the short-term enjoyment of the moment has been followed, almost inevitably, by having to deal with a complaint at the end of the service.

A congregation without music may be a good idea. I'd love it. It would enable us to concentrate on a whole different tranche of problems. Anybody else in?

We can also get a bit scared of silence. 'A few moments' silence', in most churches, lasts about seven seconds. A theological student friend of mine said, 'We're going through a period in College Chapel where you can't have silence. You're only allowed to meditate if someone is playing in the background the sort of music that means somebody has died on "Neighbours".'

Once, last year, a few of us decided to say Wednesday Evening Prayer in a churchyard, as it was too nice outside to sit in a dark chapel, and so we recited the Psalms as ancient bricks witnessed. We read of Samson as builders carried substances up the path to their project. (What a blind alley revenge is. Who could imagine setting fire to foxes' tails?) We noted Paul's longing to preach the gospel where Christ was not known as we sat on walls that have known him for ages. We recited the words as swallows called in reinforcements to buzz a magpie. The traffic could have been a mile away, not the few yards that it actually was. The sun had lost its full heat but was delightful in the way that it can be only on a Somerset evening. Better than candles.

'Shall we bring a bottle of wine for afterwards next week?' said the Rector. It felt as if that would be good.

Adorable worship can creep up on you like that. A sense of the numinous is not easily manipulated. But when it happens…

Moses took his sandals off. Isaiah felt despair. Shepherds were terrified. None of them had a bowl full of God's wrath emptied in front of them. (Trust me, you probably wouldn't want that to happen as it happened in the 16th chapter of John's revelation-dream.) All responded with some sort of worship.

'Hallelujah, for our Lord God Almighty reigns. Let us rejoice and be glad and give him glory!' (Revelation 19:6b–7a)

I have said all this because I want you to be able to strike a balance between knowing what helps you to worship God, alone and in company, and knowing how you can help others with their choices.

Here's a problem. The children are in church and the first song is an action song. You don't like action songs. But, for the sake of togetherness, will you join in? Or will you stand there in an 'I shall not be moved' way with that ridiculous expression on your face? I've seen it and, trust me, it's stupid.

How well other people join in with the things you like will be related to how you join in with the things you don't like.

I once brokered a conversation between a youth worker and a vicar. I was standing at the back of church with pre-service organ music playing gently. 'I can't stand this music—it does my head in,' said the youth worker. The following week, I was standing in the same place at the beginning of a youth service. Some pumping jungle drum and bass was coming over the PA and the lights were dimmed. 'I can't stand this music—it does my head in,' said the vicar. Exactly the same words.

I took the vicar and youth worker to each other and told them to have a conversation. It was a short one but I think they began to understand something of the other's head.

What did we say earlier about finding a perfect church? To summarise: you won't.

You may feel very down about this. Your church is not an easy place to worship God, and you would really rather leave than stay—leave for the more lively and vibrant worshipping community down the road or in the next town.

One thought before you go. The grass is greener on the other side. Either it rains more there or they built their lawn over the leaky septic tank. Hesitate long and hard.

You can keep going in a straight line by keeping your eyes on a fixed point. It's how people learned to plough. The Christian, whatever the circumstances, keeps her or his eyes on the fixed point of Jesus.

To those who are impatient with the stuffiness of their traditional church: 'If you want more life, give your life; if you want more prayer, give your prayer; if you want more love, give your love.'[9]

How do we take this advice? We go to Jesus again, via a New Testament letter.

Paul and Timothy's joint letter to the Philippians is encouraging. It is a thank-you letter first and foremost. The Philippians are a group of believers who have been generous to Paul—generous in prayer and practical giving. From his first visit there, recorded in Acts 16, it was the rich (like Lydia, a merchant trading in fine cloth) who were converted and whose resources were used to support Paul's ministry from then on. The letter shows his gratitude: 'You sent me aid again and again when I was in need' (Philippians 4:16b).

Paul and Timothy have been at pains to set out in chapter 1 that, although Paul is now in chains, this is in no way a hindrance to the gospel. How can he be accused of preaching Christ out of selfish ambition if he has been locked up for doing it, and continuing to do it will not hasten his release?

Paul has now heard that the Philippians are also suffering, and he wants to encourage them and help them to cope.

Chapter 2 is a special piece of the Bible for me. It begins with a word that is missing from most of our Bibles. In Greek, the first word of 2:1 is 'So' or 'Therefore'. It warns us that Paul is writing on the basis of what he has argued so far—and then he launches into four great 'Ifs': 'If you have any encouragement from being united in Christ, if any comfort from his love, if any fellowship with the Spirit, if any tenderness and compassion…'

So, do you? The attitude Paul is going to describe is only for those who can say 'Yes' to all these questions. And if you can? If you can say 'Yes' to them all, then… 'be like-minded' (2:2a).

Like-minded with whom? With Paul? With each other? With God? Well, yes, but get the order right. If we all strive to have God's mind, to see things more from his point of view, then we will be more like each other. The more we are like God, the more we will be like-minded (if we are all trying to do it) with each other, and the more we will have 'the same love, being one in spirit and purpose' (v. 2b).

To this end, wouldn't the church be great if we all managed to 'consider others better than yourselves' (v. 3b)?

We can't be who Jesus was but maybe we can do as Jesus did. And what did he do?

[Jesus], being in very nature God,
did not consider equality with God something to be used to his own advantage;
rather, he made himself nothing
by taking the very nature of a servant,
being made in human likeness.

And being found in appearance as a human being,
he humbled himself
by becoming obedient to death—
even death on a cross!

Therefore God exalted him to the highest place
and gave him the name that is above every name,
that at the name of Jesus every knee should bow,
in heaven and on earth and under the earth,
and every tongue acknowledge that Jesus Christ is Lord,
to the glory of God the Father. (Philippians 2:6–11, TNIV)

These verses have a lovely pattern to them. We start at the top, work down and back up again. A willingness to take on true humility is what we have as our example.

How do we do that? How do we follow the servant-king? I guess we follow as people who sometimes lose their way, sometimes find the route too hard, sometimes can't keep up, but always remember that he is the one we are trying to follow. I don't find it particularly easy, being a follower of Jesus; sometimes I don't know precisely where he went. But my general aim on the whole of life's journey is sorted enough that, even though from time to time we seem to be separated, I can usually find him again. No, that's wrong. It feels more as if he usually finds me again.

This also says to me the last word on suffering. We don't have a God who turns his back on suffering—one who started the world going and then left it to its own devices. We have a God who identifies with the worst of it all. There is a cross at the lowest point of my graph. In the middle of human history is an event around which we date everything.

So, after this glorious hymn to Christ (which may well have been an early Christian hymn that Paul dropped into his letter), we have some practical outworking. You see, it is all well and good to be obedient when the boss is around, but how about when he's not there? Have you 'always obeyed—not only in my presence, but now much more in my absence' (Philippians 2:12)?

Have you done 'everything without grumbling or arguing' (v. 14)? The words used here are, literally, 'murmurings' (pretending obedience but talking behind the boss's back) and 'disputings' (arguing about petty differences).

We may sometimes feel that we don't know where Jesus went, but we have the cross to tell us where he's been. If we go back there (as the church's calendar helps us to do), we can pick up the trail.

In May 2011, as the Palestinian political parties were trying to take the first tentative steps towards unity, a concert was held on the Gaza Strip and Mozart was played. 'For a moment,' said one audience member, 'I felt I was part of the world.' The right music, at the right time and in the right place, can do that.

On other occasions there may not be an exact fit. Once, an artist was asked what his abstract painting meant. He replied, 'If I knew what it meant I would have said it, not painted it.'

Do we struggle too much for clarity? Does it matter very much if we offer some things in worship when we are not precisely sure what we are doing or why we are doing it? If it is all intended for the greater glory of God, he can probably cope.

If you are a part of a small, traditional community, singing canticles you don't much care for, led by a choir whose best years are behind them, you are still uniting in the eternal song of heaven. You may just need to get in the habit of worshipping not with your ears but with your ears covered.

If heaven is like the book of Revelation, I may have my ears covered for a long time. It's not my scene. Many rock musicians over the years have threatened to leave heaven for the other venue if they could not have their guitars with them.

I have listened to the many scientists involved in the experiment to recreate conditions just after the Big Bang, using the CERN particle accelerator. What comes over is not so much an understanding of exactly what they are doing, what they will observe and how, but more the sheer excitement of it all, to them. Countdowns, applause and champagne all communicate that this experiment is important, exciting and difficult.

For those of us who feel that we already have a good take on the meaning of life, with the particle accelerator simply adding to the sum of human knowledge about it, there's a lesson here. Perhaps more excitement, applause and champagne would convince people that we were serious.

The language of theology, although sometimes necessary for the sake of clarity among initiates, is not easy for outsiders to follow. The language of excitement is—which is why the Alabama 3's claim for their music, quoted at the head of this chapter, catches our attention.

It's Sunday. 10.00 a.m.

'Welcome. We are going to be in touch with the creator and sustainer of the universe in 5, 4, 3, 2, 1…'. I can almost hear the pop of the champagne corks now.

Pause for thought

We are going to be in touch with the creator and sustainer of the universe. Wow.

Discussion questions

- With which of the five senses do you worship most comfortably?
- What would your ideal act of corporate worship be like?

Prayer

Lord, help me to worship you in spirit and in truth.

Intercessions

They devoted themselves to the apostles' teaching and to fellowship, to the breaking of bread and to prayer.
ACTS 2:42

'I'm just sick of all the poison. The drip drip drip of slagging off and cheap cracks and judgements of people we don't know and the endless nastiness of it all. It makes me want to have a bath.'
KATIE CARR IN *HOW TO BE GOOD* BY NICK HORNBY [10]

A world-famous evangelist stayed at my house for a week. He asked me what I thought of Mrs Thatcher, the then Prime Minister. I probably went off on one. He let me go. Then he asked, 'Do you pray for her?'

Truth be told, I probably prayed for her to have an accident. I was suitably rebuked. Jesus called us to love our enemies and I wanted the leader of my country to have misfortune. No marks. Start again.

If there is one thing that you can do as a member of the church without anyone being able to stop you, it is pray. Many of the great revivals in church history have, sitting behind them, the stories of faithful people praying and praying for years and years and years.

What preceded Jesus? Many years of Old Testament prophecy of a Messiah, of course. But Luke goes out of his way to give due note to two people who had been praying for almost ever:

Now there was a man in Jerusalem called Simeon, who was righteous and devout. He was waiting for the consolation of Israel, and the Holy Spirit was upon him. (Luke 2:25)

There was also a prophet, Anna… She was very old; she had lived with her husband seven years after her marriage, and then was a widow until she was eighty-four. She never left the temple but worshipped night and day, fasting and praying. (vv. 36–37)

These people lived with the unfulfilled prophecies of the Old Testament. In Hebrew (the language of the Old Testament) the word translated 'wait' can also mean 'rest', 'stay', 'trust' and 'hope'. There are huge swathes of time in the history of God in which the best thing to do, the best thing, is to wait. To wait properly. Not fidgeting or impatiently but quietly and gently.

Simeon and Anna understood this. They were pre-Christian but part of our Christian history and heritage. They were waiting for the Messiah—and in their old age, what they had been waiting for happened. They would probably both have died before Jesus reached puberty, but they knew everything was going to be all right.

One of my heroes was a guy called Ruben Gonzales. He's dead now. He was the pianist with the Buena Vista Social Club, a tea-dance band from Cuba, discovered in the mid 1990s by US guitarist and songwriter Ry Cooder. Cooder worked with them on an album that became a bestseller and the band eventually performed at the Carnegie Hall. Gonzales' motto, as he stepped into the limelight at the age of 70-something (no one know his true age), was 'You never know when your flower will bloom.'

Don't you love him?

Are you in a dull church? Your flower not bloomed yet? Wait. In the meantime, do what you do, and hope, trust and, of course, pray. If necessary, for 60 years—or longer. We will find out why one day, but it seems clear that God likes this sort of behaviour.

The beginning of the film *Gladiator* is amazing. We are introduced first to a fearsome and terrifying bunch of barbarians, then to the Roman army. They quietly and carefully prepare. Their efficiency and modern techniques—aerial bombardment, interlocked shields, moving as a unit—are going to win the day.

In the final chapter of the letter to the Ephesians, the writer compares the pray-er to a warrior and uses the effective armour and weaponry of a Roman soldier as an illustration.

Ephesians is a letter to a dearly loved church. Paul's farewell speech to the Ephesian elders in Acts 20 is incredibly moving. He may not, many experts say, have penned this letter with his own hand but his sentiments drip through it. Paul never stopped praying for the Ephesians and for everyone else he knew who got the letter. And we've now got it, although it has arrived a couple of thousand years late.

The earlier chapters in Ephesians have lots to do with relationships. Paul's dearly loved church included thieves, those who spoke bitterly, liars, those who talked dirty, angry people, loud people and rude people (4:25–31). Nothing like us, then.

So how does Paul end his letter? Well, if there was ever any doubt that this life is a battle, Ephesians 6:10–18 is a famous passage about equipping ourselves to deal with the reality of everyday living: put on your armour.

I've often thought that a visit to Tesco at peak time would be considerably enhanced by the provision of body armour and a substantial weapon, but I don't think that's quite what the letter means. In this passage, all the bits of armour are metaphorical—they stand for something else—and the battle is a spiritual one.

There is evil in our world: 'the powers of this dark world and... the spiritual forces of evil' (6:12b). Although it is often invisible, it is real enough. So how does the well-dressed Christian (now there's a laugh) get kitted out for a morning's spiritual warfare? Let's get dressed.

'Finally, be strong in the Lord and in his mighty power' (v. 10). That word 'finally' tells us the letter is coming to an end. (We can see that, but if you were listening to the letter being read, it might come as a relief.) 'Finally, be strong...' The Greek is passive: it means 'be made strong'. Allow strength from somewhere else to come to you. And it uses the word *dunamis*, from which we get our word 'dynamite'.

While it is wrong to read our word back into the original, it is good to think of getting some dynamite inside us as the sort of power we are talking about. Of God's power we should expect nothing less.

How are we to be made strong? 'Put on the full armour' (vv. 11, 13).

A few years ago, playing that stupid game cricket, I broke my ankle while batting. Before walking on to the field, I had gone into the pavilion and put on gloves to protect my hands, a thigh pad to protect my thigh, an arm guard to protect my arm, a box to protect whatever I put in it, and two pads to protect my legs. I also wore cricket boots and thick socks. (I'm not a very good batsman and I've seen how much protection the good ones wear.)

The pad on my left leg slipped round somehow during the walk from the pavilion, and the first ball I faced hit me full on the left ankle. As my partner called for a leg bye (don't worry about what this is—it meant I had to run), I realised that as I ran my leg was getting shorter. Ouch.

To protect yourself against a cricket ball, you need all the armour in the right place or you spend the next few weeks on crutches.

So, as we go through this list of armour from Ephesians 6, don't tick the pieces off too complacently, saying 'I do that' or 'I've got that'. Look out for the armour that has slipped a bit and is not protecting you. You will need to stand firm (it says, three times) in any war against evil. It is easy for your standards to slip a bit.

Let's look.

'Stand firm, then, with the belt of truth buckled round your waist' (v. 14a). 'Belt of truth' is a poor translation. It means a girdle. This is where we gird up our loins. Before you could put armour on, all your undergarments needed to be bound together. For the Christian in a spiritual battle, the undergirding is truth.

If you always tell the truth, it makes your life easier because you don't have to remember what you said and who you said it to. There's a whole chapter on this in my previous book, *Mustard Seed Shavings*.[11]

Truth as default is a challenge. It's well worth working at. It holds everything else together.

'With the breastplate of righteousness in place' (v. 14b). This isn't about a spiritual holiness but about the here and now—about doing what is right.

'To neglect what we know to be a righteous action is to leave a gaping hole in our armour.'[12] The breastplate covers an area where we are especially vulnerable and where an injury may well be serious or fatal. Christians should do the right thing. We often disagree about what is right but I'm sure God is more concerned with motivation than results.

I don't like battle and I don't like battle images. Jesus didn't fight. So the third piece of equipment is one that appeals: '... and with your feet fitted with the readiness that comes from the gospel of peace' (v. 15).

I like the idea of good news shoes. I often mistype 'god' for 'good', and I find it amusing and hard to correct. God news shoes, indeed. News of God in your very shoes.

'How beautiful on the mountains are the feet of those who bring good news' (Isaiah 52:7a). As the possessor of probably the world's ugliest feet, I am encouraged by this verse.

Shoes give you a firm footing. Even in the midst of what is described as a battle, we can have inner peace and a gospel of reconciliation and peace. All this gear just to tell people to stop fighting. We know that a peace-keeping force is often in danger and needs its protection. We should be a peace-keeping force in the world. It is sadly a valid criticism of many 'religions'—yes, Christianity included—that they lead to war, not peace.

'Take up the shield of faith, with which you can extinguish all the flaming arrows of the evil one' (v. 16). Sometimes only faith is good enough. For people of real and deep faith, the opposition can often be cruel. A big faith, in this extended picture, is like a big shield. It protects against distant enemies and unexpected enemies that you cannot see.

The 'flaming arrows of the evil one' probably means words. Trickery with words is a tactic that evil has used since the world began, as recorded in the Genesis story, spoken by a snake: 'Did God really say...?' (Genesis 3:1). They are the most powerful evil words ever.

Words burn and destroy. There's no need for them to do so, faithful people. Deflector shields up, Trekkies. With your shield available, you might not easily be goaded into an argument but you'll be sure you have understood the other person first.

If you have ever been approached by someone who's angry, it is wonderfully deflating to respond not with equal vehemence but with 'You sound quite upset. Could you tell me some more? Shall we go and get a coffee?'

That's how the shield is meant to work.

'Take the helmet of salvation...' (v. 17a). Many folk get quite uptight about our living in a nanny state. They would prefer to ride their motorbikes without wearing crash helmets. The late Linda Smith, a superb comedian (everyone I've quoted in this chapter seems to be dead: nothing personal), suggested that we are so wary these days, you probably have to do a risk assessment to eat a live yoghurt.

This piece of armour is not about risk assessment—a new trouble for many of us in our daily lives, with which we have had to come to grips. It is about confidence.

You would probably ride your motor bike more carefully if you didn't have a helmet on. It might even lead to complacency to wear one. But in battle a helmet enables you to go on the attack without fear. It gives you confidence. The helmet is about confidence, not complacency; about assurance of your fate. You are saved.

'... And the sword of the Spirit, which is the word of God' (v. 17b); 'For the word of God is living and active. Sharper than any double-edged sword...' (Hebrews 4:12a). The Romans used short, two-edged swords. Their weapons were efficient.

Jesus used God's word as his weapon against the devil when tempted (see Matthew 4:1–10). Each temptation was met with a quote from Deuteronomy. If you know your Bible, you will find it easier to defend yourself in this spiritual battle. The word of God should inform you that spiritual battles can be won.

After the armour in Ephesians 6 come the tactics, and we should note them carefully. In your not-quite-perfect church, you are still waiting, hoping and trusting for things to happen. 'And pray in the Spirit on all occasions with all kinds of prayers and requests. With this in mind, be alert and always keep on praying for all the saints' (v. 18).

'Lord I'm ready for battle on your behalf. What do you want me to do?' This would be a good prayer to pray. Be on your guard. You never know when your enemy might strike or your opportunity might come.

Put the armour on. Without getting dressed each day, we are Christian streakers, deliberately tackling life in the nude. Everyone will laugh at us.

I told you that I don't like battles. A few years ago (with apologies to those who don't like their scripture adulterated), I had a go at rewriting this passage to keep the sentiment but change the image. It went like this.

Finally, be cool in the Lord, the King of cool. Put on all the oomph going so that you can face evil with confidence. This is not just a human thing. If you are frightened of muggers in dark alleyways, take the light way home. Spiritual opposition is more subtle. So be prepared. And ready for whatever.

Being honest is like keeping your trousers on. It should be obvious. Only take your trousers off if they are really holding you back.

Don't let anything get into your heart that will spoil your relationship with the one who made it.

Know your Jesus stories. Like pride in a good pair of new trainers, let people notice and wonder where you got them.

Hold your beliefs firmly and sincerely if people are chucking random bits of pseudo-religious nonsense at you, but be prepared to put them down for a while when the chatter is calm and seeking after truth.

Know your eternal future in your head and keep a hat on in winter. You lose a lot of heat through the top of your body.

Wise people compiled books of words they thought they heard God saying and things they thought they saw God doing. Wiser people still sorted them out and put them together. If you meet people who haven't read these words, try and help them. It's easier than trying to listen to God's voice directly, and you don't have to go up a mountain to do it.

Give God feedback pretty much all the time. It sometimes feels like he's not listening, but enough people think he is for it to be worth the risk. What harm can it do? While you're at it, ask him to help others who are seeking after the truth too.

That's Ephesians 6:10–18 without a battle or a weapon in sight, and with apologies to Eugene Peterson, who does this sort of thing in THE MESSAGE with more aplomb.

So you are ready and waiting. You are not in charge. You are praying.

How about doing an assessment of where your church is right now? I'm going to teach you to do a five-point audit of your own church. It was taught to me by the late Mark Ashton in the 1980s, and I have carried it round with me when visiting churches ever since.

It involves answering five questions:

- Is the power of prayer the mainstay of our work?
- Is the Bible the backbone of our teaching programme?
- Is the gospel the central attraction of our work?
- Are individual relationships key in the way our church is pastored?
- Is the fellowship of the church the necessary context for Christian growth?

If you belong to a small group, house group or study group, they would make interesting discussion questions. If you come to any conclusions, why not share them with your church leaders?

Finally in this chapter, what can you do if your major gifting seems to be in prayer? Many times in acts of corporate worship, meetings and other gatherings, you will need to learn how to pray when someone else is speaking. Your 'Amen' ('So be it') is what makes the pray-er's prayer your prayer.

Encourage others when they pray, and offer them feedback. How rare it is for anyone to go out of their way to thank the intercessor for well-thought-out or well-prepared prayers. If you are able to take your turn on a rota for intercessions in church, then plan and prepare well.

Try to balance praying for the home team with praying for others. Also, balance praying for your own nation with praying for different countries. There are other balances too:

- Needs and thanksgiving.
- Specific and general.
- Newsworthy and less remarkable.
- Silence and wordiness.

I value a number of people who lead intercessions in my church, and I am grateful that they are not all the same. I recall a comment from one member of the church that the reason she joined us, when she moved into the area, was that our church was not inward-looking but prayed a lot for others.

Offering ministry for others is best done with the authority of the church. Again, at the church I belong to, we spend time praying before the meeting and see if there is anything particular God wants to say to the congregation. Sometimes these thoughts, pictures or ideas are little more than a hunch. On other occasions we get them clearly. Either way, we set them before the people for testing.

Three specific people who have been called to a ministry of intercession are available after our worship to pray with others. Often the 'words from the Lord' are the nudge that people need, to ask for prayer. If you feel drawn to praying for others, find out how your church can use your ministry.

Let's end big. Could you start praying for a BHAG—a Big Hairy Audacious Goal? (Thanks to Coventry Diocesan

Missioner Roger Morris for introducing me to this idea.)

Think of an example of something that might happen but couldn't happen without God. A growth in numbers of 100 a week without any change in our activity. An outrageously generous response to a gift day.

Go on. Dare to dream.

Pause for thought

In yachting, as I understand it, the mainstay holds everything else up. That's what prayer does.

Discussion questions

- **Has any of your armour slipped a bit?**
- **Have you concentrated so much on defence that you have nothing to fight with?**
- **Do you get dressed each day spiritually as well as physically?**

Prayer

Lord, teach me to pray, as Jesus taught his disciples.

— ❖ —

5

Not just me

Certain individuals came down from Judea to Antioch and were teaching the believers: 'Unless you are circumcised, according to the custom taught by Moses, you cannot be saved.' This brought Paul and Barnabas into sharp dispute and debate with them.
ACTS 15:1–2A (TNIV)

Bureaucracy always overcomes vision; it's a tragedy. But stories will undermine bureaucracy.
PHILIP PULLMAN [13]

You can see from the opening passage that in the very early days of the church there were disagreements. Fairly substantial ones at that, if you happened to have a penis. Read on in Acts if you want to know what happened, while I uncross my legs.

Disagreements are normal. Churches should expect there to be differences of opinion. What should set aside the church from the rest of society are the grace, openness, honesty and mercy that temper our dispute-handling. Was that cloud cuckoo land I was visiting then? Sorry.

A wise vicar friend of mine was approached by a member of the congregation one day. 'I don't like the way <name> is running our 11–14s work' was the gist of the complaint.

'Have you told her?' asked the vicar.

'No, I'm telling you so you can sort it out,' was the response.

The vicar responded in the negative, gently pointing the

complainer to the many verses in the New Testament that show how we should bear with one another, sort things out with one another, confront one another and be accountable to one another, and how taking things to arbitration was seen as a last resort, not a first.

You may feel a little powerless in your church. I hope you don't but I know it happens. Some church leaders are a bit autocratic, even tyrannical. There are many who delegate but some who don't. There are some who abdicate but many who don't.

If you are a member of a church, how do you support your leader? Well, first you pray for them. Second, you encourage them as specifically as possible. Third, if necessary, you confront them when you think they are wrong. In other words, do exactly the same as you would hope your leader would do to support you.

How might you go about disagreeing with your leader? Not all people are good at receiving criticism. I am of the opinion that my eight years in the claims department of a leading insurance company gave me the ability to accept criticism. My job was to make the unhappy happy. Go and work in customer service for a while, then tell me if you still mind negative feedback.

All I can say to those of you who have a bone to pick with your minister is to do it from the right motive, if possible with a smile on your face and at a convenient time.

On the one occasion when I and another member of a church felt that a senior minister needed to be confronted, we chose to write a detailed letter and ask for an appointment to discuss it. We were told off not for the content but for our timing. The church was involved in an outreach project at the time, and the minister thought we were wrong to discourage him right then.

Perhaps you could pre-warn: 'I've got one or two things I'd love to talk through with you and I wonder when might be convenient and free from interruption', followed by, 'Would you like me to give you an idea of what these things are in a brief note beforehand?'

On other occasions, I have had the response, 'It was not what you said; it was how you said it.' I think self-awareness is a rare gift—to know how you come across to others. By God's grace I am slowly improving but I know I am an intimidating character to many folk. Often, after getting to know me, they discover that I am simply blunt and speak my mind. I try to speak less of my mind in the first few seconds after meeting someone than I used to. Otherwise, I may mean well but it doesn't always sound as if I do.

Do you sometimes mismatch what you say with the way you say it? Dare you ask someone to tell you?

How do you get to contribute your ideas? There are several ways—meetings, working groups, sub-committees, feedback, notes, emails, texts, conversations over coffee. Try to match the seriousness of what you have to say with the method by which you say it.

If you have to say something critical of your leader, it might be useful to take soundings from others first. It's just possible your leader might be right.

I don't want to defend the clergy and other church leaders too much but I have to say that ten seconds after I've walked out of the church building, having preached an expository sermon, is not the best time for me to hear that I need to sort out the ticket arrangement for next month's concert. Could you leave it a minute or two?

Let's hear it for Martin, an unsung hero in my life. After our church morning worship, he brings me a coffee. He knows I get involved in serious conversation with people at this time and often fail to get in the coffee queue at all. He brings one over. It is a lovely thing to do.

I think I give criticism due weight when it comes from those who are not always critical. And not so much when it comes from those who are.

I once heard the evangelist J. John speaking to a gathering of youth groups from around the country. It would have been about 1986. He said the Christian life was easy: 'Just do what God tells you to do.' He used that phrase as a mantra throughout his talk. 'Just do what God tells you to do.'

He was right. But how easy is it? In the early part of the book of Revelation there are letters to some churches—in Ephesus, Smyrna, Pergamum, Thyatira, Sardis, Philadelphia and Laodicea. These were, presumably, places that tried to do what God told them to do. How do we know that? Because they were churches and that's what churches try to do.

Think of all the threats these new and fragile Christian communities were facing—threats that came about because they forsook their first love (as in Ephesus), were terrified of the idea of suffering for Jesus (as in Smyrna), were compromising their faith (as in Pergamum) or were tolerating false teaching (as in Thyatira).

The letters to the churches came to John, the writer of Revelation, in a vision and he was given the script of letters he had to write. He addressed them not to church leaders but to each church's 'angel'. This seems to be deliberate. The 'angel' of the church may literally mean its guardian angel or, as some have said, it may represent the church's ethos or personality.

'Revelation' and the alternative title of the book, 'Apocalypse', come from the Latin and Greek words for 'unveiling'. When you unveil something (as in the old tradition of a bride's veil being removed at the moment of marriage), then the picture becomes clearer. You can see. Michael Wilcock, in his commentary, says that we must see Revelation as a 'glorious picture book' given to us as a balance to the history of Luke and the theology of Paul.[14]

We must have in mind, then, that whenever we read Revelation we are reading words that were designed to make things clearer. In places where they don't do that, we must ask ourselves, 'What's changed? What has happened in 2000 years of history to make this apparently obvious thing obscure to us?' Then we will be equipped to read the book.

I want us to look at the fifth letter, the one written to Sardis. Sardis had a few of the problems we will have if we don't get the focus right in our churches. The letter to Sardis tells us what the ordinary Christian should be thinking about.

Sardis had become more worried about reputation than salvation. In the first four letters, the churches have all had something to commend them. Not so Sardis. It only has a reputation for being alive: 'I know your deeds; you have a reputation of being alive, but you are dead. Wake up!' (Revelation 3:12).

Tough language. Fancy only being alive by reputation.

After a first curacy in Nottingham, my family and I moved to County Durham to work in the parish church in Chester-le-Street for five years. I probably made light of it, because I do, but I was a bit scared. Chester-le-Street had a remarkable recent history of growth and church planting. I had read a whole chapter about it in a book, which said:

There are now six separate venues for worship under the auspices of the Anglican church on a Sunday morning. There are a further two services at the church building during the day, another two during the week, and one more monthly service in a local community building. On a good week the total can be around a thousand people at worship.[15]

A thousand people? I was terrified—until I got there and I met them. They were a wonderful, mainly working-class community of ordinary people whom God had blessed remarkably. I loved my time there. These people didn't care a jot about their reputation. Most of them hadn't read *Ten Growing Churches* and had little idea that they were famous. Certainly the youth group, with whom I spent a lot of time, were too young to know about their history.

Later, I had another experience as I went to work for an organisation that I'd supported for years. The Church Pastoral Aid Society was, as far as I could see, full of bright, innovative thinkers, movers and shakers. That they would offer me a job with the youth team was a great privilege. I was apprehensive. Had I been too cocky at interview and led them to think I was as good as the rest of them? I now felt inadequate.

Again I found that, while everyone was especially good at their job, this was also a place where folk bickered about the coffee rota, irritated each other by making too much noise in an open-plan office and didn't agree (amazingly) about the best way of gingering up the church's youth ministry at the end of a decade in which the church had lost 300 teenagers a week. But it was another job that I loved. It kept me on my toes. It stopped me bluffing. It taught me to write and train.

Reputations can be quite problematic. They walk into the room before you. Do not worry about your reputation, like Sardis did.

There is a second problem with being dead: the command 'Wake up!' is not that useful. The dead tend not to.

So we need to see the problem at Sardis as this: they are not doing what God wants them to do, but they are convincing everyone except God that they are.

My friend used to sell workstations for a computer giant. He had a frightening monthly target. Many of his colleagues would nibble away at their target, selling a thousand here and a thousand there. Not so my friend. Once, with two hours to go on deadline day for monthly reports, everyone else was finishing the final small deal to hit their target while my friend was trying to nail the one deal that would bring in double his target. Otherwise his monthly figure was going to be zero.

He took the call agreeing the deal as the Managing Director was being shown around. 'You lucky git,' shouted his colleagues, on hold to various secretaries around the world. 'Who?' said the MD. 'Bring me the lucky one. I like lucky people in my organisation.'

It's a great story and I vouch for its truth.

The boss commends the risk-taker. When you take risks, you *know* you are awake. You don't have to be told.

In his book *Thriving on Chaos*, business guru Tom Peters tells how he commended a manager who had just delivered a good project. When the manager asked, 'What next?' Peters gave the answer, 'Something great'.[16]

Go and do me something great. Take risks.

There is a huge lesson for me from Sardis. Being the leader of a medium-sized church is the easiest job in the world if you pastor simply by being nice to people. Everyone will speak highly of you and your reputation in the diocese will be good, especially if you keep paying your parish share and don't do anything unwise with someone other than your wife or husband.

Once you start suggesting walking on water, though—huge spending projects, massive campaigns to invite friends, moving things on, (gasp) change—the work becomes awkward. Also, your reputation as a leader in the diocese can change because you become the subject of complaint to senior staff. But that way also lies church growth—in discipleship by trying new things, and numerically by reaching new people.

I don't imagine your church is dead like Sardis. But the way to that sort of death is not horrid: it is nice. It is the death into an easy life.

Having an easy life, in this letter, is said to be like soiling your clothes (see v. 4), whereas we would think that lazy people had the cleaner clothes. In Revelation, whiteness is an image of holiness. The harder you work for the Lord and the more risks you take, the more you step out in faith and the whiter your metaphorical robes become.

The motto of my old insurance claims department was 'If

the boss comes round, try not to look busy.'[17] The quieter the claims department was, the more money the company was making.

I love the old film *The Great Race*. Hero Tony Curtis breezes through a giant pie fight, only taking one hit, towards the end. His clothes are otherwise clean. In the film he is the good guy: he keeps himself clean. John's letter commends those who get stuck in. This church's disobedience is about their inactivity.

Sardis had to learn that if the Lord came and found them having an easy life, that would be bad: 'If you do not wake up, I will come like a thief, and you will not know at what time I will come to you' (v. 3b). They were also more worried about the immediate than the long-term.

What is the gospel about? In this passage, it is about bums on pews on the last day—getting as many names in that book of life as possible. On the way we may feed the hungry, visit the lonely, help the poor, clothe the naked and even heal the sick, but the point—the whole point—is not food, company, money, clothes or health, but eternity. (I know there are other Bible passages that balance this viewpoint: we need to hear both.)

In the other letters in Revelation, churches are promised rewards; all Sardis gets promised is that if they turn things around now, their names will not be deleted from the book of life.

Sardis had a citadel. It was huge and was never taken by force. It was, however, taken by stealth a couple of times. John wanted to remind the church that the Lord would come like a thief. He would judge when they least expected it—perhaps by stealth, not force.

This image of the thief is important. Paul used it: 'For you know very well that the day of the Lord will come like a thief in the night' (1 Thessalonians 5:2). Luke also used it: 'But understand this: if the owner of the house had known at what hour the thief was coming, he would not have let his house be broken into' (Luke 12:39). (You know something is important if you find it in the Gospels, Paul's letters *and* the book of Revelation.)

Sardis had also had a devastating earthquake, in AD17, maybe some 50 years before this letter was written. People living in the city would have known what it was like to experience sudden and unexpected catastrophe. These things can happen. The long-term view sees them as inevitable but potentially distracting from the bigger picture.

Might a church be so wrapped up in its own short-term projects that it forgets to put alongside them (alongside, not instead of them) the salvation of outsiders? Never forget the job of witnessing, whatever the state of your church leadership. Being in the long-term business is about looking to Jesus' return, not the end of the current church project. Get your name, and others' names, in the book of life. That is long-term and urgent work.

Sardis was also more worried about starting than finishing: 'Strengthen what remains and is about to die, for I have not found your deeds complete in the sight of my God' (v. 2).

Some people in Sardis had got it—people who still recalled their first response to the gospel, people whose righteousness was unstained. They knew that the adventure of following Jesus has only one finishing line—not baptism, not confirmation, not marriage, not children, not retirement, which are all points at which people can tend to opt out of the Christian life—but death.

The one with the spirits and the stars in his hand, who speaks to angels, is the one who equips the church to do his will. To have another go when feeling disheartened. To be encouraged when feeling scared. To trust that God is in it all, however bad it might be, personally, right now.

'Just do what God tells you to do.' How does that work in your church?

The Church of England is part of the one, holy, catholic and apostolic church. It is episcopally led and synodically governed, and if you think that sounds like a dodgy compromise, find someone else to take it up with. I may make fun of the rules but I don't make them up.

The Synodical Government Measure of 1969 (sometimes I amaze myself with how much useless stuff I actually know) was designed to give the laity (non-clergy) more say in the running of the church. Good show, say I.

So bishops are in charge but often complain about their relative powerlessness to do anything. Some, such as the current Archbishop of York, manage to make powerful and symbolic statements with word and deed; others work behind the scenes through political process. Hierarchical synods sort out the nitty-gritty of policy, so we have General Synod (which meets three times a year and normally makes the telly), Diocesan Synods, Deanery Synods and then the Parochial Church Councils, which often moan about their relative powerlessness to get things done.

Hypothetically, a PCC could pass a motion that the Deanery Synod reps could put on their synod agenda to discuss, vote on and pass on up the line. So the ordinary person has access to the power structure to get things done, subject to lots of democratic checks and balances. It works but it is painstaking. That self-same ordinary person can also stand for election to the higher synods.

You may not be a leader but you can get involved in this stuff at every level. If you are Church of England and want to know a bit more about how your rectors and vicars come to you, then look at www.churchsociety.org/issues_new/churchlocal/patronage/iss_churchlocal_patronage_history.asp

How are other denominations run?
To find out a bit more about how the Baptist Church works in the UK, go to www.baptist.org.uk/how-the-union-works.html. Methodists are governed by Conference. Find out more at www.methodist.org.uk/index.cfm?fuseaction=opentogod.content&cmid=122. For Vineyard Churches, see www.vineyardchurches.org.uk/about-vineyard-churches.html. Others are easily Googleable.

We all live our lives by various rules. As I drive home along the spine road of my anonymous suburban housing estate, a large flashing sign illuminates, should my speed dare creep up to 31mph. It's the rules. Then there are disciplines—self-imposed rules such as not leaving dirty washing on the floor or studying the Bible *before* the racing form.

What rules are we subject to? The law of the land; local by-laws; employment contracts that we have agreed to ('I do this and you pay that'). Some rules remain on the statute books but have passed into obscurity and are only dragged out to be laughed at, such as:

- It is illegal to die in the Houses of Parliament.
- It is legal to murder a Scotsman within the ancient city walls of York, but only if he is carrying a bow and arrow.
- In the UK a pregnant woman can legally relieve herself anywhere she wants, including in a policeman's helmet.
- Wolverhampton Wanderers supporters can legally be taunted in April.

So there. (I made one of these up.)

In the New Testament, we see people being defensive about rules. Jesus upset the scribes and Pharisees by his apparent lack of respect for laws. Matthew wrote his Gospel from the perspective of one defending the law (of Moses). Paul wrote in Romans 13 of the need to submit to the authorities, whom he describes as God-given.

Much has been made recently of the centuries-old dilemma of distinguishing between the historical Jesus and the Christ of faith. Philip Pullman's novel *The Good Man Jesus and the Scoundrel Christ* has got it going again, helpfully.[18] But is the church, as Pullman might put it, an organisation running totally contrary to the spirit of its accidental founder, and designed to control people?

It can be. Those of us with leadership responsibilities have to take seriously the need to empower, not disenfranchise, the people we lead.

Looking through the Canons of the Church of England recently (I obviously have too much time on my hands), I found many rules that I habitually break—rules to do with my mode of dress, the content of the church services I lead and my pattern of daily prayer. I break them willingly, deliberately and with the view that not breaking them would be detrimental to the growth of the church, which the spirit of the Canons is designed to promote, not hinder.

If you architects want to know where to put the footpaths on a new housing estate, do not build any until people have lived there for six months. Then look at where they have trodden the grass down, and put the paths there. Rules, in many circumstances, should not restrict behaviour but should describe it. So let's build some new paths. Let legislation catch up with reality.

That might take time and be easier said than done, of course. Last time a motion was put before General Synod to relax the rule about the wearing of robes by clergy, it was thrown out. Democracy has arranged things so that the small number of churches that are growing—by and large, the robeless ones—are not able to carry a majority on synod. So the status quo is voted for by the majority of synod people, who like their clergy robed. Likewise, for the relaxing of the formality of Eucharistic Prayers in church.

I don't robe at Trendlewood Church, I often don't even wear a dog collar, and we have invented a form of Eucharistic Prayer that the children can use. Lock me up.

Recently, US author Anne Rice quit being a Christian, a fact that she apparently displayed on her Facebook page. She was quoted in *The Guardian* as saying that in the name of Christ she refuses to be anti-gay, anti-feminist or anti-artificial birth control. (Ah, a Roman Catholic Christian, then, we deduce from the final 'anti'.) She also refuses to be anti-Democrat and anti-secular humanism, anti-science and anti-life. That's one crazy, mixed-up leaver, is it not?

It is interesting how 'Christian', once upon a time a nickname for a bunch of weirdos who got Judaism wrong, is now the name of a huge worldwide religious phenomenon including some weirdos who get Jesus wrong.

I reassert my desire to remain within whatever it is that is being described when we talk of the church, and to affirm from within that I will do all I can to be Christ-like toward gays, women, scientists, condom wearers, Democrats and humanists (which may include finding some of the things representatives of these groupings say, to be wrong).

Anne Rice is right to say, as she does, that Christ is infinitely more important than Christianity, but once you exclude yourself from the fellowship of others who also believe he came that we might have life to the full, you either have to start a sect of the like-minded or be a solitary Jesus-follower, something unknown in the New Testament.

The things on your list of gripes may be slightly or substantially different from Anne's and from mine, but we are all on the same side. As I have to remind myself when passing the appalling street preachers in Bristol City Centre who scattergun passers by with phrases that get lost in the wind, I probably believe some of the same things as these people do.

Is there a blueprint for fixing disputes? There is, but you won't like it.

I once got into trouble with some colleagues for suggesting that cross-carrying be included in a church manager's job description. I was just saying that a job description for ministry—'lay down your life in the service of others'—is never going to be popular but we do need reminding of it.

Jesus was brought before Pilate:

Pilate then went back inside the palace, summoned Jesus and asked him, 'Are you the king of the Jews?' 'Is that your own idea,' Jesus asked, 'or did others talk to you about me?' 'Am I a Jew?' Pilate replied. 'It was your people and your chief priests who handed you over to me. What is it you have done?' (John 18:33–35)

Whichever Gospel you read, it will strike you very hard that Jesus could have saved himself with a more cautious use of words. His decision to continue being mysterious and obscure seems odd to those of us who would have saved our lives, given half a chance.

Pilate had no idea what was going on. Writing much later, after Jesus' death and resurrection, the apostle Peter (who had denied Jesus three times, we recall) said this: 'He himself bore our sins in his body on the tree, so that we might die to sins and live for righteousness; by his wounds you have been healed' (1 Peter 2:24).

Jesus did not retaliate. He took what was coming. Peter says that he bore it in our place. Dramatic stuff. In fact, it's a great story—which, as Philip Pullman knows (see the quote at the start of this chapter), trumps bureaucracy every time.

Christians should not be doormats on which everyone wipes their feet, but there is no shame in sacrifice for the sake of others. It's the principle on which our faith is founded.

The local leaders had trouble with Jesus' leadership. That's interesting, because Jesus didn't spend much time claiming leadership. He just taught. He healed occasionally. But one of the best tests of whether you are a leader or not is to turn around and see if anyone is following you. Jesus had followers; therefore he was a leader.

One day the chief priests and teachers of the law came up

to Jesus and asked him straight: 'Tell us by what authority you are doing these things... Who gave you this authority?' (Luke 20:2). He asked them a question back: 'John's baptism —was it from heaven, or from men?' (v. 4).

It was a clever response. Was anything supernatural going on through John the Baptist? The priests and teachers couldn't say 'From heaven' or Jesus would ask why they hadn't believed him. But they couldn't say 'From men' because the people thought John had been a prophet and would turn on them. Who'd have thought the chief priests and teachers of the law would turn out just to be a bunch of people-pleasers after all?

'So they answered, "We don't know where it was from"' (v. 7). Those teachers were all for truth, as long as it wasn't costly. Christians need to be in the truth business—the costly truth business. That's how you settle disputes. You seek after truth without assuming that you have it and the other person doesn't.

That leaves us with these few questions.

How should a church make a big decision? At what point should the elected representatives hold a referendum? What majority at such a vote would represent a mandate? At what point is a decision big enough to need a vote by the elected representatives rather than a call by the executives? Which decisions need referring to all the people?

Is this issue all about whom we should trust? The rector? The church wardens? The elders? The church council? A small voice crying in the wilderness? A small person crying in the corner? Or should we draw lots? These are all thoroughly biblical things to do. Let me know when you've got an answer.

You see, the truth of Jesus will apply to different circumstances differently. Told you you wouldn't like it.

Pause for thought

Say to yourself, 'I am an important part of the Christian church in <name> and I will play my part.'

Discussion questions

- How do you feel about arguments and disputes?
- What was the last big dispute you got involved in? How was it resolved?

Prayer

Lord, help me to seek after the truth of your gospel and apply it to my life.

— ❖ —

The state of the coffee

So the Twelve gathered all the disciples together and said, 'It would not be right for us to neglect the ministry of the word of God in order to wait on tables. Brothers, choose seven men from among you who are known to be full of the Spirit and wisdom. We will turn this responsibility over to them.'
ACTS 6:2–3

I would say that most of the ecclesiastical wardrobe and historical buildings are a hindrance to effecting much contact with the community.
JOHN WIMBER [19]

I have a theory about ecclesiastical tableware generation. All church hall kitchens are fitted with a crockery and utensil magnet. However, it is powered by a complex Boggle-o-matic device (named after the scoring system in the game Boggle, in which only original words score points), which ensures that only one of each type is attracted or retained. After a period of a few years, no item of church kitchen crockery or cutlery matches any other.

Is this a good witness? Do you think this would happen if the people in charge of the church hall kitchen were full of the Holy Spirit and wisdom?

A guy in a church I attended was great with names. He met people one week and remembered who they were next week, instantly. We put him on the door. He wasn't so good at the conversation after next, so we tried to keep him on welcome and newcomers. Did I mention that he was the vicar? Great witness. Great first port of call. And the church? He organised it so that others could take things from there.

A member of my current church is not that good at remembering names, but she loves people and has a smile that makes the world feel good. We put her on the door. She tends to be so concerned about people that she over-commits unless we keep her focused on welcome and newcomers. Did I mention that she was my wife? Great witness. Great first port of call. And the church? We organise it so that others can take things from there.

Two very different people but with a gift in common of welcoming and putting people at their ease. Get the hospitable to hosp. They'll love it. It will work.

A church not a million miles away from where I live was recently in vacancy, and it was expected that a number of prospective clergy would be visiting informally to suss everyone out. It was amazing how enthusiastic the members of that church became about welcome and hospitality at that point.

So why is your coffee rubbish? Could you, as a small offering to your community, make it your job to improve the state of the coffee after church? In a world where a good coffee is less than half a mile away from 75 per cent of the population (I made that up, by the way), it should be possible to arrange for a church to offer real stuff.

This is important. It will take twelve times longer to turn a church round than it will take to turn the coffee quality round. Changing the coffee changes an attitude. We begin to think about offering a stranger the best, for free.

I don't know if you are the victim of unenthusiastic preaching or worship leading. I'm sorry if you are, but I want you to know that, regardless of this, you can still welcome newcomers. In fact, your welcome becomes all the more important, because, from time to time, Christians will be moved around the country due to their employment and will be looking for another church. Many of them, if mature in their faith, will be looking for a church where they can serve, help and generally get stuck in. The quality of your hospitality may convince them that there is life beyond your minister's preaching skills.

All church members are in the hospitality business. It is essential that everyone is on the look-out for the stranger. Imagine if you were feeling lost, lonely or depressed and, on a whim, wandered into a church service to see if there was anything there for you. If you hadn't been before, or for a long time, it might all be a bit strange. Someone might hand you a load of books or pieces of paper. Or perhaps this church projects everything on to a screen, so you don't get the comfort of having anything to hold. Either way, it is good to have a cheery person to offer help if needed.

I went to church as a small child but rebelled as soon as I could. I told my mum it was boring. Between the ages of about six and 16, I went to two funerals and a wedding. I think my primary school might have taken us along to a church at Christmas, Harvest, Easter or some combination. All I can remember is that when I knelt down, as instructed, I couldn't see anything over the pews.

When I was 16, someone invited me to a youth service at my local church, the same church that had been boring all those years before. I don't quite know why, to this day, but I went along. Perhaps it was the possibility of (whisper it) girls being there.

I was amazed. It was full of ordinary young people, having fun and being welcoming. I started attending the youth group meeting and the next week I went to church again. It was a bit empty when I got there, so I sat at the front. I didn't know you didn't do that. I thought I had nabbed the best seats to see the drama or the short film—although, come to think of it, where had the projector screen gone?

When the service started, it was much more like the sort I recalled from my childhood. A robed choir, chanted responses and psalms, old hymns and language that suddenly swooped into Latin as we sang the Nunc Dimittis or Magnificat. I felt it would be embarrassing to run for it, as I was at the front and everyone would look at me, so I stuck it out. No one sat within three rows of me, so I had to look over my shoulder every now and again to see if I was meant to be standing or sitting.

The thing that kept me? The only thing that held me there? Relationships. After the service I got chatting to the young people I had met the previous week. They had been sitting at the back. They explained why church wasn't like the youth service every week.

Following up newcomers is obviously essential. Your church needs a system for capturing the names and addresses of those who are new. Could you make this happen? Your church needs to be able to follow up newcomers with a friendly visit to explain what else is on offer. Could you do this? Your church needs its communications to be easy to read and crystal-clear. Are you good at this sort of thing?

And someone, anyone, needs to make sure that old

notices are taken off the noticeboard the second they are out of date. And those notices that are ragged and a permanent fixture on the board? Take them down after ten days. You have my permission to attack your church's noticeboard with vehemence. I'll take the blame. Tear up anything that's been there more than a month. No one is reading it.

If there are legal documents that need to stay there, put them on a separate board behind a locked glass panel.

That got a bit ranty. Sorry. But why is this important?

'And the Lord added to their number daily those who were being saved' (Acts 2:47b). The Lord adds to the number. He added daily to a church that had recently baptised 3000 new converts.

You are the best advert your church has. God grows your church. You don't do it. But if God sees you planning to improve your welcome, you should expect him to send you some people to practise on. There may not be time to buy 3000 matching coffee cups but you can still smile.

How strange is the Church of England? Don't answer. I'm going to tell you. Imagining myself as a stranger to the system, even though I am a friend of the family, I went to a Cathedral Church for the Licensing, Collation and Installation of a new archdeacon. Name any other major event that happens at 5.15pm unless so arranged by Sky Sports.

The cathedral was a beautiful building, totally spoiled by the modern addition of a huge and ghastly organ in the middle, blocking the view of the far end. The decision to hold the bulk of the archdeaconing ceremony on the other side of the organ, so that the guests (apart from a select few) could hear but not see, was remarkable. At one point a voice gloated, 'You can't see me but I can see you.' My neighbour told me it was Vincent Price. Hanky-in-mouth time.

I am not a great fan of organ music, apart from a bit of early Emerson, Lake and Palmer, and I spent most of the service longing for the noise of bass, drums and electric guitar (not just the music of my youth but the music of my life) or the clever use of a small choral sample with a break-beat. The PA system forced every speaker to communicate slowly and made most of them sound evil: 'Take the archdeacon to the sanctuary—see that some harm comes to him.'

On arrival, I had failed to observe a walking-stick leaning against the back of the chair I chose. The stick fell over when I sat down. Jesus heals the lame but this guest knocks over their sticks.

I would have liked a bit of explanation from time to time. Why was the Archdeacon given true, actual and corporeal possession of his seat, and what would have been the disadvantage if he had only received two of the three possessions? When was the Titular Prebend of Yatton annexed and by whom? Were we supposed to get him back? What was the Prebendary Ball, and could anyone have a kick? Why did the two Bishops choose that precise moment (the first line of 'Crown him with many crowns') to put their mitres on?

Would it have been so very hard to do the ceremony where we could see it, explain what was going on, and have some responses in with which we could join (as the C of E might put it)?

I tell you this because I know what it is like to be a stranger. It does me good. It reminds me that even when the dignitaries are having fun with long words, a bit of a welcome from someone who is in on the plot can be wonderfully helpful.

Someone wise once said that you only have one chance to make a first impression. You are bound, some day, to be a stranger's first impression of your church. Now, did you choose to come to church wearing a fleece with food down it? Did you park near the church so that you wouldn't have to walk far, but now the stranger must? Did you catch the newcomer's eye and then look away and look down? Yes? You blew your chance. The first impression is now fixed.

And those complex words? Let me rewrite what we do, so that it sounds as strange to us as it does to visitors.

The church comes into the church to commemorate the death of someone who is still alive. The one who is still alive isn't there, and a person stands up and invites everyone who is already there to come into the presence of the one who was dead and is alive and isn't there.

On a table is a loaf of bread and a bottle of wine. But the bread isn't bread; it is the body of the one who isn't there. And the wine isn't wine but the blood of the one who isn't there. But they are still bread and still wine and still look and taste like bread and wine, even when the person who said 'Come into the presence of the one who was dead but is alive and isn't there' says they are now blood and body.

The bread is food but not for those who are hungry. The wine is drink but not for those who are thirsty. The hungry and thirsty should eat and drink before they arrive.

The bread needs to be broken in order to work. If it isn't broken it won't work. The person who breaks the bread says, 'We break this bread to share in the body of the one who was dead' but this is not cannibalism or violence.

Everyone is invited to share in the bread but some churches won't let go of the cup to let this happen with the wine. Although the bread and wine are the most important bits of this ritual, the cups and plates are treated as more valuable. Some churches use funny bread which sticks to your dentures.

When everyone has eaten and drunk a little bit, they go in peace to love and serve the Lord. They do this by drinking coffee and talking about each other.

Some people like to eat bread and drink wine to remember the dead one every day. Some only do it on special occasions. Some still don't remember the dead one, however often they do it. Others never do it but don't forget the dead one. This is not because wine makes you forget.

Did you get that? Your church is odd. Always remember that. Odd.

In the summer season at St Paul's Leamington Spa, where I used to minister, numbers didn't take a massive dip. The regular morning 280 became about 200; the evening 80 went down to 60. But there were usually up to 50 different faces—people popping back to see family, tourists, and other visitors.

One morning, one of the visitors was a child aged perhaps 8 or 9. He was wearing an immaculate creamy white suit, shirt and tie. He came out to the front and waved flags during the singing. In a short gap between two songs, he heckled, 'Play the next song' from right behind where I was standing. After the service he came and tried out the Reader's Desk (the place where the church service leader sits) that I had been using, as if planning to be doing it himself some day.

I had no idea who he was or whose he was. Later, over lunch with friends, I discovered that this child had only been to church once before, and that was to a wedding. When he heard that his family were planning to go to church, he put on his wedding clothes, imagining that everyone else would, too.

If you have only one experience of something, it is very hard to persuade yourself that all parallel experiences are not identical. But go through a church door these days, somewhere in this country on a Sunday morning, and no two visits will be the same.

If you are in the business of retaining people's custom or support, you may think that the best thing to do is to give them occasional outstanding service, content or offers. While these things are not bad ideas, they will not necessarily do the job. It is consistency that makes people return. So the way to retain business is not to have one-off acts of genius but to eliminate all the acts of folly.

Retail research tells us that one in 100 of the people who have a good experience in your church will tell a friend. But one in ten of the people who have a bad experience will tell a friend. So if you don't fix the leaks, you will have to have ten times more genius than error, simply in order not to shrink.

Eliminate the bad experiences. Every welcomer needs to be on their game 100 per cent, all the time. Few people notice a clean church; loads notice a dirty one. Hardly anyone comments when the temperature is just right; lots will tell you if it is too cold and some when it is too hot. Ever overheard, 'That service was exactly the right length, Vicar'? Not often, I'll warrant. But the opposite? Oh yes.

It comes down to detail. 'Who sweeps a room as for thy laws makes that and the action fine,' wrote George Herbert.[20] Indeed—but only if you are consistently good at sweeping.

It follows that the boss/leader/chief/minister/vicar/pastor should handle all complaints personally, if possible one-on-one, and take them seriously. That way, it reduces the damage.

Eliminate errors before attempting greatness. This applies to your football team's defence, a shop's customer service, the beer standard in your local, and my preaching, equally.

Let's go back to Stephen Cottrell's quote from the beginning of Chapter 1: 'The problem with Christianity in this country is that there are too many churches; the Gospel paradox is that the solution is to build more.'

Why is this true? Too many of the churches are in the wrong place, and too many of the smaller gatherings in those places are stuck in the past. So a minister, trying to grow the local church, may find it easier to plant a totally new congregation than to encourage an existing one to be genuinely welcoming to the alien and stranger. This might mean investing minimal effort in keeping a small congregation of the unchanging and unwelcoming going, and maximum effort in working out what to set up that will attract others.

David Jenkins, former Bishop of Durham, once told a group of us that he had been advised that if a small, former pit-village church closed, the congregation would not go elsewhere. His reply, which I can still recall pretty much word-for-word, was 'Fancy even considering, even considering, keeping a church open where the congregation had learned so little of what it was to be church that they would not go to another one if theirs closed.'

He may have had poor publicity from time to time but he was a wise man, for sure.

So, another hospitality question. How smelly are you? The greater number of senses that are involved, the more powerful will be the memory. Think of perfume counters. They're often by the front door in department stores. Why? Because that memory will get fixed. 'It smells good here. I'll be back.'

I used to go for a drink with my dad at the local pub in summer. We sat in the garden. I had lemonade with a straw. He had a pint. We sat near the extractor unit from the bar. That smell of stale air, cigarette smoke and beer comes to me on the air from time to time, and I think of my dad, without fail. Smell is a very powerful memory-jerker.

Paul's letter to the Philippians is about hospitality, and the final chapter is about smell, or fragrance.

- It is a letter to a church that has had to be told to keep its eyes on the fixed point of Jesus, in order to get everything else going in the right direction.
- It is a letter that calls its readers to the example of the service and humility of Jesus, on whose death the whole of human time is hinged.
- It is a letter to a generous church, which has supported Paul in his work.
- It is a letter that has told us of the need to be willing to export our best people.

So how smelly are you? Get these things right and you will be a hospitable bunch of Christians.

There's much more in Philippians, I know, but this is one application only. The nub of it is in the final chapter, a chapter we tend to gloss over because it seems to be mainly full of greetings and special messages and people with funny names.

'I plead with Euodia and I plead with Syntyche to agree with each other in the Lord' (4:2). What was it like to fall out over something and be mentioned in Paul's letter? What had these two women, Euodia and Syntyche, fallen out about? We don't know. What we do know is that a public dispute between Christians, not managed 'in the Lord', will bring disrepute to the church. It is the opposite of hospitality. It puts people off.

Paul sees disunity as a disaster. He probably knows what caused the argument, but he does not do detail. He pleads with them to sort it.

In my favourite ever TV series, 'The West Wing', President Bartlett, towards the end of his period of office, is faced with a problem. Two states are arguing over which one has responsibility for a train crash: it happened near the border. The President asks for the governors to be brought to the phone. We cut to the phone call. 'Governor, we need to sort this thing,' says Bartlett, 'Get it fixed.' (We don't hear the reply.) 'Thank you, sir.'

An aide asks the President which governor he was speaking to. The President says he has no idea. It didn't matter. The problem needed sorting and anyone could make the first move. Euodia or Syntyche? Who cares?

'Someone else's problem' is the antithesis of hospitality. A church surrounded by overflowing dustbins because nobody thought to get them emptied won't attract strangers.

'Just sort it, Governor.'

'Yes, Mr President.'

We serve a higher power than the President.

Paul throws a quick-fire list at the Philippians and, via them, at us.

- Are you content in all circumstances?
- Are you anxious?
- What occupies your thought-life?
- How prayerful are you?

These things, if we get them wrong, distract us from our mission of welcome.

Paul thanks the Philippians for their gifts to him. They've obviously sent him money. This leads to a reminder: 'The gifts you sent… are a fragrant offering, an acceptable sacrifice, pleasing to God' (v. 18b).

In an environment where people still used the sacrificial system, the smell of burning meat would have been clearly known to Paul's readers. When our worship, our behaviour, our attitude or our generosity pleases God, Paul says it is like an acceptable sacrifice.

We have lost the idea that God might be pleased by the smell of a burning pigeon (that's what Paul would have had in his mind), but the illustration remains. The understanding of Jesus' sacrifice was putting an end to burnt offerings, but smells leave strong memories. 'Your generosity has burned itself on my memory.' What a witness.

The Japanese dish Natto achieves something quite remarkable. It is a dish that is unpleasant to all five of the senses. It looks disgusting, like regurgitated porridge with green pesto. It smells ghastly. As you remove a spoonful of it from the bowl, a squelchy noise can be heard, not unlike pulling a wellie out of mud. To the tongue it feels like wallpaper paste with tadpoles in it. It tastes of very little with added salt. I will never forget it.

Now how can we become so hospitable that we make our churches attractive to all five senses?

Pause for thought

Try to be a fragrant offering to the Lord this week.

Discussion questions

- Well? How can we make our churches attractive to all five senses?
- What part can you play in your church's hospitality industry?
- Do you smell of Jesus?

Prayer

Lord, as I try to meet the needs of others, please meet all my needs according to your glorious riches in Christ Jesus. (Based on Philippians 4:19)

Sunday special?

Consequently, you are no longer foreigners and aliens, but fellow citizens with God's people and members of God's household, built on the foundation of the apostles and prophets, with Christ Jesus himself as the chief cornerstone.
EPHESIANS 2:19–20

One of the unspoken rules of squats… is that you generally have to let people do what they want within reason.
JOY PRESS [21]

Back in the 1980s, as the government of the day eased up the regulations, to allow trade and commerce to happen seven days a week, there was a campaign to 'Keep Sunday Special'.

Well, that ship has sailed. The campaign might have had a chance if people had felt that the church had something better to offer than shopping, but, with all retail outlets closed except paper shops and off-licences, the 'Keep Sunday Special' campaign was seen as 'Keep Sunday Dull'.

For many Christians, church is still an organisation with a Sunday focus—the Lord's people meeting on the Lord's day. More recent converts or enquirers may have found that it was the work of a church on the other days of the week that attracted them—a discussion group, a men's night in a pub, an Alpha course on a midweek evening.

In whatever way people become captivated by a desire to be part of the church, we are now more wary than ever of suggesting that 'proper' church is the Sunday meeting. We have also found—as do those in squat accommodation, according to Joy Press's piece—that people are less and less fond of rules that restrict voluntary behaviour.

Why on earth shouldn't the midweek Mothers' Union meeting be church for those who attend? They pray. They worship. They hear input based on God's word. Each term they have a Communion service. They care for their sick, take up an offering and look for new members. What's not church about that?

Or take a monthly event that I hold. I live in a quiet part of town in a big house. Once a month, it is my privilege to throw open the doors for up to twelve people to join me for a day's quiet. We read the Bible at the start of the day and take a couple of Bible chapters to ponder (if we haven't brought along anything else to wrestle with). We talk over a meal at lunch-time. One of my regular guests comes to this event, and this one only, during the month. It is her church.

When the Church of England started becoming inventive with liturgy in the 1960s, some new expressions found their way into the *Alternative Service Book 1980* and then its successor *Common Worship*.

Back in the Prayer Book days, we had described praising God as 'meet, right and our bounden duty'. In the new liturgies, which were already well in use by the time I joined a church, this phrase had become:

It is indeed right,
it is our duty and our joy,
at all times and in all places
to give you thanks and praise.
COMMON WORSHIP

Duty and joy—that covers it for me.

Many of the themes of church will be found in the letter to the Ephesian Christians. We have already looked at the end of Ephesians, where the armour of Christ is discussed. Now we go back to the beginning and think about being a community of grace. This is often the opening sentiment of many New Testament letters: 'Grace and peace to you from God our Father and the Lord Jesus Christ' (Ephesians 1:2).

Ephesus was a large city, maybe with a population of a quarter of a million. It was the capital of the chief province of Asia Minor, a mile or so from the sea. It was a financial and banking centre. The temple of Diana (also known as Artemis) was important to commerce and attracted pilgrims.

Paul pitched up there on a missionary journey. A silversmith named Demetrius made silver shrines of Artemis. His livelihood was producing souvenirs, and Paul was saying that handmade gods were not gods. Demetrius called a union meeting of the silversmiths' guild and said:

'Men, you know we receive a good income from this business. And you see and hear how this fellow Paul has convinced and led astray large numbers of people here in Ephesus and in practically the whole province of Asia. He says that man-made gods are no gods at all. There is a danger not only that our trade will lose its good name, but also that the temple of the great goddess Artemis will be discredited.' (Acts 19:25–27)

He started a riot.

Paul eventually spent three years in Ephesus, longer than he spent anywhere else, I believe. Passing by later, he called the leaders of the Ephesian church to him and said, 'You know how I lived the whole time I was with you, from the first day I came into the province of Asia' (20:18b).

'You know how I lived.' You bet they did. 'From the first day I came.' How could they forget? And the letter that bears his name sends grace and peace.

It's an example to us all. As a Christian, your example is important—even if it causes a riot from time to time.

Ephesians 1 is a reminder of where people stand in Christ. Take some time out to look at all the once-and-for-all verbs in verses 3–14. They're things that have been done, remain done and won't need doing again. These verses are all one sentence in Greek.

Why am I telling you this? We'll get there. Hang on a bit longer.

The letter moves on to prayers for the people who might be reached by the letter. (Ephesians 1:15–23 is another single long sentence in Greek.) Paul prays 'for the Spirit of wisdom and revelation, so that you may know him better… that the eyes of your heart may be enlightened' (vv. 17–18). These are things that we too may ask for, as we duplicate the prayer.

So what is in this for you and your church? The passage reminds us that it is all about Jesus: God's purpose is 'to bring all things in heaven and earth together under one head, even Christ… God placed all things under his feet and appointed him to be head over everything for the church' (vv. 10, 22). Things come together under Jesus.

In Michael Cole's little book *He Is Lord*,[22] he tells the story of a journey taken by one church, to make Jesus Lord of everything—to reestablish him on his throne, if you like.

Cole felt that a local church that made Jesus Lord of everything would be dramatically transformed. One of the many fine things he observed was, 'Today, sadly, many Christians are living sub-normal lives, so that we have come to accept the sub-normal as normal.'

People who are not experiencing the presence and power of the risen Lord Jesus at work in their lives by his Spirit may well have settled for second-best. This is sad, because the best is only a prayer away.

I have met a lot of fantastically gifted people in churches. Almost all are very busy. They're busy doing wonderful, Christ-like things such as feeding hungry people, looking after elderly relatives and running parts of church life—and these things are done in spare time when busy days at work are over.

One question: is Jesus Lord of all this activity? Is there a still, small voice whispering in the background, saying, 'Slow down, do less, retire early, go part-time'? How loudly would Jesus have to speak for us to hear him say, 'Don't spend so much time at work... feeding the hungry... with your family...'?

I have no insight at all that he is saying those things to anyone, just a nagging feeling that a church won't grow if we are too busy to make friends and expand our circle of contacts. Until there are enough people doing this in my church, I will see it as a major calling on my time.

My ordination did not bring me into a new job. It meant that the church freed me from the necessity to have a job in order to serve the Lord full-time. That is why my money is called a stipend (compensation for not having a pay-packet), not a salary.

Why am I telling you this? Nearly there. One old joke first.

A guy falls from a roof and is left clinging to a window-ledge. 'If there's anyone up there, help me!' he shouts. 'If there's a God in heaven, have mercy.'

'Throw yourself down and I will take your weight,' says a booming voice from the heavens.

The guy pauses for a moment, then shouts, 'Is there anyone else up there?'

You see, we speak to God but we don't expect the voice that answers back. We go to church but we don't expect to hear the creator and sustainer of the universe there. Maybe he isn't there. Perhaps he didn't get welcomed or doesn't like the coffee.

Mark Greene, Director of the London Institute for Contemporary Christianity, writes:

I'm convinced that we are missing something, that the message of the gospel is being partially eclipsed and that this has led to a narrower, less radical, less adventurous understanding of what it means to follow Jesus than the Bible's compelling picture.[23]

His booklet is a reminder that, while we celebrate Sundays, the Christian life is about every hour of every day of every week. It's the reason why I have teased and taunted you with the point I might eventually make—which is this:

Church meetings last, say, two hours if you include travelling and waiting time—some more, some less. But there are 166 other hours in the week that are *just as important*. That's why Demetrius and his gang in Ephesus were so uptight about the gospel. It was going to mess up their day jobs.

In many churches, everyone is very faithful, everyone is very busy, but (dare we say it?) somehow everything is a little comfortable. Where are the false starts, the failed projects, the risky words, the journeys into the unknown?

What happened after the riot in Ephesus? Paul wanted to go in there. His friends thought he'd be lynched, so he agreed not to. Then the nominated representative of Paul failed to get a word in. The uproar died down. Paul looked at that, thought 'Okey dokey', and left them to it. 'You know how I lived the whole time.' Yeah, Paul, we know.

Church services, meetings and acts of worship should be equipping Christ's people to live for him the other 166 hours of the week. Exactly how they do it is unimportant. If you miss church, will your church miss you? Yes, I would hope so—because they will want to know how the rest of your life, your real life, your 166 hours, is going. And you will feel the same about them.

If you have no church as yet, the question of how to choose a church arises. My theory is simple. If you are a new Christian, get advice about the nearest church that will feed you. If you have made a commitment to a particular denomination (sect of the Christian church), then go to the nearest church of that type. If not, then go to the nearest church. In all, get stuck in, offer to serve, make friends, and leave if there is any suggestion that Jesus is not welcome or not Lord there.

You need to be in the company of people who make Jesus Lord of their lives if he is going to remain Lord of yours.

In the James Bond film *Casino Royale*, there is a wonderful opening chase scene involving free-running on a building site. The two actors fight and play pursuit along beams, scaffolding, tower cranes and many other sorts of industrial paraphernalia.

It is said that a break was called in the middle of the scene, while one of the two stunt doubles was on the arm of a crane. Rather than climbing down and going for lunch, he stood and waited for two hours or so until the team returned. I get dizzy just looking over the edge of my bed. I feel sick thinking about that story.

The stunt man put his faith in his ability and training. That's the opposite of grace. Grace says that everything that needs to be done for you has been done for you. You need do nothing in your own strength or ability. Grace involves complete trust of the other, not of self.

Ready to run into the rest of the week after Sunday? Free-running after careful preparation is one thing, but free-running in Christ is an altogether riskier business.

Jump?

Pause for thought

Imagine standing on a crane jib, with a dizzying drop to the ground. Enjoy the moment. In your imagination, stand there as long as you can.

Discussion questions

- Think about the other 166 hours. Is two hours each Sunday equipping you for them?
- If so, give thanks. If not, what might need to change?

Prayer

Lord, help me to serve you beyond Sunday.

❖

How to not be a leader

Peter said to him, 'We have left everything to follow you!'
MARK 10:28

If you want to go fast, go alone. If you want to go far, go together.
OLD AFRICAN PROVERB [24]

What is the church? In various places in the Bible we will find metaphors—suggestions of what the church is like. It is like a body. It is like a family. It is like a building. It is like a temple. It is like a bride. It is like a meeting of clans.

Which one is true? Silly question. Because they are analogies, they are all true, or all contain some truth.

So you can assess the health of a church like a body.
You can assess the unity of a church like a family.
You can assess the growth of a church like a building project.
You can assess the holiness of a church like a temple.
You can assess the readiness of a church like a bride.
You can assess the size of a church like a gathering.

In some of those images, it is more clear than in others where the leader is. But which is the most important brick in a building? They are all important. Which is the most important part of the body? They can all catch a disease that will kill you. The best way is to see how Jesus-centred all these images are. In the Christian church, both leaders and members are following Jesus—together.

So, I thought (as I mentioned in the Introduction), I'd put a note out to the blogosphere and see if anyone had anything to say concerning what should be in a book about not being a leader. Here is a selection from the replies I received:

- How to avoid volunteering for things you don't actually want to do.
- Why leaders shouldn't bother trying to guilt-trip people into doing stuff.
- Being creative followers...
  - coherently diverse
  - helpfully subversive
  - persuadably political
  - tentatively assertive

This last one was really interesting, so I followed it up with the writer and talked about some work she'd done on the subject. I will be spending many a long hour working out how to be tentatively assertive, if that's all right with the rest of you.

There were more suggestions:

- What to do when your leaders tell you they've prayed about something, and are doing what they feel led to do, but you think God wants something different.
- How can parishioners ask ministers to stop intoning their prayers as if they were doing God a huge favour by praising and blessing his holy name?

Do you know how it felt to read these replies? Not as if I'd struck a seam of gold in hearing what people wanted to discuss, but as if I was having a petition handed to me by an anti-clergy protest march. We really have upset some people.

Two other comments rescued me from my slough of despond:

- Choosing a church: what matters and what doesn't?
- Are ministers leaders or facilitators of God's Spirit in action?

These are both really good questions, and I hope you will find that this book has covered them adequately. If it wasn't for them, though, I would have felt buried under negativity. All those people feeling put upon and press-ganged, hearing God more clearly than does their minister, whose style they hate.

This is not a new problem.

My brothers, some from Chloe's household have informed me that there are quarrels among you. What I mean is this: one of you says, 'I follow Paul'; another, 'I follow Apollos'; another, 'I follow Cephas'; still another, 'I follow Christ.' (1 Corinthians 1:11–12)

Now I would have expected to see Paul end this argument once and for all by saying, 'We all follow Christ, dummies.' But he doesn't—firstly because the word 'dummies' was not a term they used then, but secondly because when people respond to arguments over leadership by saying, 'I follow Christ', it's a bit like a game of cards when someone has just played a trump. 'This group is the most difficult to evaluate. Their emphasis and language are usually above reproach and their 'hot-line' to God can be very intimidating.'[25]

Membership carries responsibilities and delights. That's the joy of being part of a team.

I have a great picture in my study. It is of the pit-team at a Formula One Grand Prix. There are about 20 people, working together in seven or eight seconds of perfect unity and harmony, three times a fortnight throughout the racing season.

When it works, it is a thing of beauty. On the rare occasions when it does not, and someone gets sprayed with fuel or the person at the front gets knocked over, it is a disaster—and very dangerous. Everyone in the team has to do their job precisely or the hard-earned seconds of the driver's lead have to be recovered.

Paul knew nothing of motor racing but he knew that 'the eye cannot say to the hand, "I don't need you!" And the head cannot say to the feet, "I don't need you!"' (1 Corinthians 12:21). One body, many parts. One team, many members. Working together in harmony. Lovely.

It follows that churches will need volunteers. Churches will not run without them. Increasingly in recent days, better-off congregations have used their generosity to employ people to do jobs once done by volunteers. Churches have pastoral assistants, youth workers, children's workers, family workers, directors of music, student workers, administrators, managers, caretakers and vergers. But all these people will be managing the contributions of volunteers, who earn their livings in the marketplace and offer some of their spare time.

What about rotas? Some love them; some hate them. My personal preference is to have people with particular gifts working in their area of giftedness most of the time. But sometimes, especially in young communities and smaller churches, it becomes necessary to cover activities by rota. Throw yourself in if you can. Those chairs won't put themselves away.

One comment about leadership in passing—forgive me: 'A good leader produces a "we" out of a multiple of "I"s.'[26]

A few years back, a church administrator friend of mine had been having a gentle moan about the number of things that people suddenly expected her to do. (I may have changed her gender to protect her identity.) She was much cheered by this spoof letter she received from a couple about to be married at the church:

Dear Administrator,
Can the loo rolls in the Ladies please be changed so as to match the mothers' corsages—we really don't want them to clash. Attention to detail and all that.
There is some graffiti in the vicinity of the church—'KAYA', 'Villa' and 'Dunc loves Debs'; since no one at the wedding will be called KAYA, Debs or Duncan, can you please change this to read 'J Loves G', 'Come on the 'Loo' (after Waterloo Rugby Club) and B****** (J's family dog).
We thought it might be worth seeing if we could replicate the Pink Floyd Dark Side of the Moon stage set for during the bit where we are at the registry. Do you think we could ask R / G / ME to set up a laser show, smoke cannons, inflatable pigs, and for a large scale model aircraft to come from the back of the church and crash at the front in a pyrotechnic extravaganza? We would hope to finish the performance with a large glitterball descending from the church ceiling with several multi-coloured spotlights reflecting off it.
One more thing: can you recommend anyone to act as stage dancer, a bit like Bez from the Happy Mondays, to perform with the musicians during the gig?
We also notice the ducks, swans and geese in the park tend to fly out as and when they feel like it; do you think you could

have a quiet word with the relevant people (the local vet, the park authorities, God, Ben Fogle, Bill Oddie etc) and see if they can either be chained to the railings or, even better, taught to fly in formation, like the Red Arrows, for instance. That would be spectacular for the photos.

The river is running a bit high and is an unpleasant browny sludge colour—could you please have the level lowered, the flow a bit less torrid and, if it's possible to have the water returned to its usual bluey / clear state, then that would be great.

We thank you in anticipation,
G and J

G and J are happily married now and are two of my favourite people. Their humour kept the Administrator sane that week.

So, how do you feel about change? Embrace it at every opportunity? Hesitantly go along with it, but slowly? Say, 'Change? Here? You're joking'?

I was chatting over lunch the other day to a couple from one of our local churches. We were talking about the particular issues related to having an old church building situated away from the heart of the population that it was designed to serve. We discussed how that building was, in any event, not a good meeting space because it only had one small room off the nave that was any good for gatherings.

I pointed out the wonderful reordering of another local church, which had removed pews and installed individual seats. The couple agreed that what had been done at Holy Trinity was remarkable.

'So why not do that at <name>?' I asked. 'No,' was the gut reaction, in stereo and vehemently. I think the couple then realised that I had sneakily tricked them, and backed up a bit to 'That would be a step too far.'

Why do we invest so much of our emotional energy in things that no longer serve the purpose of what we set out to do? Pews are uncomfortable. Pews are inflexible. Pews are newcomers in most church buildings: people used to sit on the floor, or stand. Pews are also (and this is, I admit, subjective) ugly. Yet people love them, fight for them and hate the very idea of removing them. Long after <name> church is gone, the pews and the building will probably still be there. They are not sacred; they're seats.

A lovely couple at a church I worked at in Nottingham were… No, let's start again. A couple in Nottingham who I didn't really get on with that well became lovely in my eyes, and changed my mind about them utterly, when this happened.

They were contemplating how to express their preference with regard to some changes to our evening service, which was haemorrhaging people. Option A was their scene: a robed choir; more eucharistic; less informal. Yet they voted for option B. They felt it was more likely to grow the church. I don't even know if they are still with us, but God knows them and I salute them.

I understand why people resist change, but, as a member of the church, please remember to vote for a course of action that will benefit the non-members.

We need to do a bit more with Ephesians, our host and guide on our journey:

For [Christ] himself is our peace, who has made the two one and has destroyed the barrier, the dividing wall of hostility, by abolishing in his flesh the law with its commandments and regulations. (2:14–15a)

The church is the starting point for visible unity. I'll say that again. The church is the starting point for visible unity.

We are troubled in our town by the ministry of a church that comes out from Bristol, prays for young people and children on the streets and slags off the local churches for doing nothing. These people then withdraw and do nothing about follow-up. A member of this church once shouted across a supermarket car park at me that he didn't think I was saved. They are in trouble with the police for approaching children: I don't believe they have valid Criminal Records Bureau (CRB) certificates. We have had difficulty in contacting them to have a conversation, and the trouble is that ordinary people in our town think they are the church.

I am secretary of the local churches leaders' meeting. It is the best group of church leaders I have ever worked among. We set an agenda each year for what we are going to do together the following year, not in the name of one church but in the name of all of us and Christ Jesus. We are slowly but surely establishing a reputation in town that all the churches are worthwhile and can be trusted.

To Ephesians again with all haste: 'For we are God's workmanship, created in Christ Jesus to do good works, which God prepared in advance for us to do' (2:10).

Far from being a passive spectator in this cosmic drama, the church is to live a life worthy of her calling, to display the unity of the Spirit, to grow together in Christ as a unified body, and to reflect to the world God's ultimate plan for the universe, testifying to a comprehensive, all-embracing salvation in lives turned around.[27]

It seemed to be the feeling in the early church that Jesus would come back soon. But his failure to return didn't so much disappoint them as challenge them that there was still a job to do. They understood that he was now with them spiritually, not physically. In the light of Jesus' death, resurrection and ascension, the task of discipleship has now been passed on to us.

'I urge you to live a life worthy of the calling you have received' (Ephesians 4:1). Remember, this letter is addressed to the saints, not the leaders. It's for all.

'Live a life worthy of your calling.' Why? Because of Jesus' headship, and because of the unity it brings. Because of the gospel and the new approachability we have with God. Because of these things, 'live a life worthy of your calling'.

Two ministers were talking. 'How's your church going?' asked one.

'Some come irregularly. Some just come to the social meetings. Some are so late we've almost got to the coffee. Some pop in and hang around at the back for a bit, then leave.'

'Oh, that's terrible. At my church everyone is firmly converted.'

Which of these churches is likely to grow? The one with the fringe hanging around and not quite joined yet. I am committed to healthy church. That means being committed to church that has a fringe.

Ephesians 4 goes on to suggest that God gives grace to each, and special gifts to some, 'to prepare God's people for works of service, so that the body of Christ may be built up until we all reach unity' (vv. 12–13a).

You can be on the fringe. You can check everything out.

You can watch from the sidelines until you are sure. But if you want to join the community of grace, you have to get on the field of play. You have to be committed.

In explaining this idea, Ephesians 4 uses (apparently) a quote from a psalm: 'When he ascended on high, he led captives in his train and gave gifts to men' (v. 8).

Psalm 68 is about a triumphal procession. It is kingly and Davidic. It begins, 'May God arise, may his enemies be scattered; may his foes flee before him' (v. 1), and the verse 'quoted' in Ephesians actually says: 'When you ascended on high, you led captives in your train; you received gifts from men' (v. 18).

As you can see, Paul has changed the words. Usually, gifts were given to the victor and shared out among the army, even the kingdom. But the victor in Paul's version doesn't receive gifts—he doesn't need to. He simply gives them.

What are the gifts for? They are 'mean-time' gifts. They are gifts intended to grow the church. They will give us unity, knowledge, maturity and full measure (v. 13).

So what are the gifts? The named list (v. 11) focuses on the gifts that would be of use in leading a fledgling church, but a natural talent becomes a spiritual gift when it is offered in God's service, and it is clear that all gifts of service and all parts of the body need to work together.

It is difficult to get succession right in a church. For some reason, folk tend to hesitate to offer to get involved in a ministry unless there is an emergency vacancy. My technique is to have as many emergencies as possible. I encourage people to move on, up and out. I enthusiastically sponsor people to apply for more demanding ministries, elsewhere if necessary.

One of the signs of a mature congregation is its ability to export leaders. Send your best people to help others or to be trained for further ministry.

May I also encourage apprenticing. Sit alongside an experienced leader and learn from her, then take over when the time is right. Does your small group have a junior leader, to whom the baton can be passed at some point in the future? I reckon all church ministries should have an apprenticeship scheme. There are a couple of things I am doing at the moment, which would fold without me. I hate that, and I'm trying to put it right.

It follows that 'how not to be a leader' is different from 'how not to take responsibility'. You can take responsibility for something while answering to someone else. This book is a bit of a con: we aspire to a church where responsibility is so well shared that no one is not a leader of some small thing.

The main flaw in the system in my particular branch of church is the lengthy period of vacancy between senior pastors. There is no sense of a vision being handed on or honed in partnership with the next leader. It means that every time there is a new minister, the church goes through a time of feeling 'All change'—when very little should be changing if vision building and casting has been on the corporate agenda all along.

Encourage your church to have a rolling five-year plan (every year, you plan the next five). Then, if there is a vacancy at the top, you can recruit into your vision rather than importing a new one.

I would find my local church life improved greatly by the simple addition of:

- extra worship/service leaders.
- more musicians, especially a drummer.
- children's helpers to plan for succession.

Their absence doesn't make our body unhealthy; their presence might make it fitter, though.

How do you support your leaders? I don't want to list all the things that would make my life easier. I'll leave it at this: talk to your leader, about everything. Communication in churches is often criticised, yet those who play the most central part in most churches are not usually the ones who complain that they don't know what's going on. This is not because they are at every meeting (I hope) but that the more involved you become, the more interested you are in discovering things.

So one thing that makes me happy, although it is a pathetically small thing, is hearing someone ask a question about something on the notice sheet. It means they've read it.

Pause for thought

Think about all the things you are not responsible for in your church.

Discussion questions

- **What is the difference between:**
  - **management and leadership?**
  - **vision and strategy?**
  - **responsibility and command/control?**

- You may be studying this book because you don't want to be a leader. How do you feel about your non-leadership right now?

Prayer

Pray for all the people who are responsible for the things you are not responsible for.

— ❖ —

What is the church doing to my faith?

But because of his great love for us, God, who is rich in mercy, made us alive with Christ even when we were dead in transgressions—it is by grace you have been saved.
EPHESIANS 2:4–5

Above all in the cities of contemporary Britain, the Church of England is far too good to write off, far too useful to ignore, and far too bad to desert.
CHRISTOPHER IDLE IN *HOPE FOR THE CHURCH OF ENGLAND*[28]

Do you sometimes look at the established church, as reported in the press, and wonder to yourself, if only briefly, why we do this to ourselves? 'Why do we do this to each other?' was nearly the title of this book. I reckoned it was too negative.

I read regularly of cases of gross pastoral insensitivity that do not cost people their jobs or bring about any disciplinary action (though they might well in any other occupation). As a break from whatever I was doing at the time, I wondered what might constitute an action leading to the revocation of one's licence these days:

Dear Bishop,

As my permission to officiate comes up for renewal, I thought it a courtesy to inform you that I have, over the last few months, gone over to the dark side. I know my friends have always assumed that my black clerical wear was somehow sported ironically, but I have to say that the affairs of the day just don't cut the mustard when compared with that which goes bump in the night.

I hope you won't feel that my swearing due and canonical obedience to your goodlordself is compromised by undertaking to serve you jointly alongside the prince of evil and the powers that roameth the earth like a vengeful lion, but I leave it up to you to decide. If you do withdraw my permission, there is a Mothers' Union Solemn Eucharist that will require cover next Thursday.

As I said to the Area Dean the other day, the asherah pole is purely for decoration and all babies passed through hoops of burning and sulphurous fire are thereafter baptised.

Since making this slight alteration to my personal spiritual journey, I have been amazed at the new contacts I have been able to make. Midnight at the cemetery is particularly productive, pastorally.

If you wish to discuss my future, I would love to invite you round. I am usually free during the day and only serve the finest and freshest organic goat's blood. I am happy to open the curtains for the duration of your visit.

I remain your semi-obedient servant and sign as I now style myself,

B. Al Zebub (Rev Dr)

P.S. My internet service provider will from now on be Demon.

That is how I keep myself sane—by writing letters that will, usually, never see the light of day. It stops me jacking it all in. Try it. It counters the frustration caused by the fact that it is hard to get our good and positive stories into the news. Hold the front page: 'Church happy. Growing steadily.' That's probably not news.

I have explained already that I am ordained and a church leader. I am therefore aware that I have had to tread carefully not to produce a book full of instructions for church members simply to make my own life easier. That has not been my intention, but I do now want to stomp around in a minefield a bit. What about pastoral care?

Looking after people's pastoral needs is not easy. Most of the books written on the subject suggest that one pastor is unlikely to be able to look after more than 150 people. So a church leader charged with the task of growing the church and pastoring it will have to change strategy if she is successful enough to take a church beyond the 150 barrier. At that point, she will have to arrange for the pastoring to be done, rather than carrying it out for herself.

A church member in a growing church should not expect to have the minister as their own private chaplain. It is more likely that a pastoral assistant or a small-group leader will be doing that work. In fact, a church of small groups is one of the most effective types when it comes to delivering pastoral care.

If you are part of a large church, sooner or later you will need to be aware not only of who to turn to if you need pastoral support, but also of who might look to you for their support. This will enable serious cases of major illness or bereavement, where a contact with an ordained member of staff might be appropriate, to be passed on. It will save your minister from working himself into the ground by having to call on anyone the first time a sniffle appears.

Here is a message from a pastor. Despite indications to the contrary, as given by some of my super-competent colleagues, we are not mind readers. One of the best ways to get to spend some time with us is to ask for an appointment. No one ever stayed at home and moaned that the doctor didn't call if they hadn't phoned the health centre first.

I had a conversation with a member of a local church the other day. She told me she had felt very badly let down by the church when she suffered a bereavement, a few years ago. Her rector was on sabbatical and so she felt uncared for. During this conversation, she praised the marvellous help she had received from family, friends and her house group. 'Brilliant' (I thought but didn't say). 'The system worked.' But it seemed that that wasn't enough. A visit from the clergy was expected, and its absence was disappointing. If this paragraph helps one person to lower their expectations of a clerico-centric church, it will have been worth writing.

I can't remember who said this but will gladly credit it if I'm told: 'In the thrombosis of the church, the vicar is often the clot.'

The thing about reactive ministry is that it is often possible to do it in the day-time. Ministers find that their evenings fill up much quicker than their days. The sick, the bereaved and those just wanting an appointment to chat about something can be invited to come, or be visited, during the day. A totally reactive ministry is easier and almost certainly causes people to like you (for being seen as a good pastor). The trouble is, it spectacularly fails to grow the church, because the minister is spending no time with outsiders who might be invited in. These people often have jobs or other day-time commitments. 'Whatever view we take of our local incumbent, he can unfairly become the scapegoat for many ailments.'[29]

I tend to avoid books that others tell me I must read. I lost two hours of my life on *The Shack* and I've never had them back. Eventually, though, worn down by the number of Christians who told me I should, I got round to reading Philip Yancey's *What's So Amazing About Grace?* It's good. It's a one-trick-pony of a book, but it's a good trick.

We need reminding about grace. It's, er, amazing.

'Have mercy on me,' pleaded the cornered soldier.

'You don't deserve mercy,' said his opponent.

'Of course I don't,' he wriggled. 'If I deserved it, it wouldn't be mercy.'

'Good point,' said the captor, and shot him anyway. No one likes a clever-clogs.

He got what he deserved. The amazing thing about grace is that we get what we don't deserve.

'As for you, you were dead…' (Ephesians 2:1). On Gozo, an island in the Mediterranean that I know and love, every little village has a huge church. One, St John's at Xewkija (Pronounced zoo-key-year), has the fourth largest dome… in the world.

It is a mirage of success, though. Success isn't about who has the biggest dome. St John's is one of the few churches in the world where someone has been rude to me, as a sightseer. Ephesus' temple to the goddess Diana was four times bigger than the Parthenon in Athens. That spoke loudly but was meaningless.

Ephesians starts with a reminder to its readers that Jesus' death was the key ingredient in God's recipe for the whole of creation. In him God has chosen us, forgiven us, adopted us, revealed his plan to us and given us the Spirit. And 'for this reason' (1:15) the writer never stopped praying for the Ephesians and everyone else he knew who would get the letter.

The difference between living with God and living without God is as radical as the dead coming back to life. 'You were dead…'.

If you are a Christian, a follower of Jesus, then you believe in a God of grace. So are there lots of gods and the God of grace is the best one? No. Can you be a Christian and believe in a God who is different—perhaps remote and awesome rather than intimate and personal? No. That would be a false god. If you live a good Christian life, will you deserve more from God than someone who doesn't? No. Some of us find it quite hard to get our heads round all that.

The God and Father of our Lord Jesus Christ, the only true God, is a God who has taken all the initiative in saving us. We are saved by the grace of God—by his kindness. God loves us, cares for us and sent his Son to die for us, and, although he wants a response of good works, he takes the risk that he will be ignored or will get no response except 'thank you'. And that is enough for him to do it—to send his Son to die for us. 'Thank you.'

I don't know what kind of a sinner you are. I'm quite a good one, managing all sorts of ways of sinning that you can't imagine, beyond the rather obvious ones that those of you who know me can see. I'm not going to list stuff now.

And the things I do wrong—the things that spoil my relationship with God and separate me from him—kill me. It is as if my relationship with God is dead in the water. I cannot live like this and expect God to enjoy watching it happen—

the God who made me and had other intentions for me.

'You were dead... But...' (Ephesians 2:1, 4). The amazing thing about grace is that it is conditionless love. If we only have conditional love from God, think about the problems.

'God loves us if...' How many ways could we complete that sentence? How would we know if we had completed it God's way? And how many small steps would we take along the path of understanding that sentence before we reached a religious teacher who encouraged us to give our lives for that god and fly a plane into an office building, or blow ourselves up on an early morning school bus, with the promise of paradise with many virgins to follow. That is what a god might be like who needs to be pleased by our actions.

'What have I done to deserve this?' We often hear this question on the lips of sufferers, especially those who feel they are suffering undeservedly. Sometimes there is a clear relationship: those who suffer in prison because of their crimes know full well what they have done to deserve it. There is a relationship between sin and suffering, but it is a complex one—so complex that sometimes we cannot see the connection at all, especially, for instance, when children suffer.

So it comes as something of a shock to discover that the Bible's teaching is that the ultimate suffering, death, is what we all deserve because of our sins. Harsh? Indeed. True? I believe so. 'As for you, you were dead...'

But the other side of the coin is that when things are going well, you've done nothing to deserve that, either. You're a lottery winner and nothing else. And the best news of all—that death need not be the end and you can go on living afterwards, only more so—you've done nothing to deserve it. Neither have I.

So what is this grace like?

Amazing grace, how sweet the sound
That saved a wretch like me.
I once was lost but now am found,
Was blind but now I see.
JOHN NEWTON (1779)

It's like being saved when you were falling, being found when you were lost, being given your sight back when you were blind. It's like that.

There is no such thing as cheap grace. It was very expensive: it cost Jesus his life. But there is no grave to visit, not even some mysterious place that came to be known as his final resting place. He's alive. We can be, too. It was expensive to him but free to us—if we want it.

Grace gives us a special position: 'God raised us up with Christ and seated us with him in the heavenly realms' (Ephesians 2:6). Seated next to Christ. Get that. And this special position gives us access to 'the incomparable riches of his grace, expressed in his kindness to us in Christ Jesus' (v. 7).

It's as if everything good in this life is only a foreshadowing of what will be good in the life to come. It is beyond compare. And, as we saw in the last chapter, it brings unique opportunities. This touches on the relationship between grace and action.

There is stuff to do, but it is a consequence of grace. It is evidence of grace. We should believe the good news so much that we are prepared to do something about it, but we don't have to. We're still saved, even if we do nothing. I wish that 80 per cent of the jobs in the church weren't done by 20 per cent of the people. I wish 80 per cent of the money the church is given wasn't given by 20 per cent of the people. I wish that people acted more saved. I know that I should act more saved myself. I really should.

What is all this doing to my faith?

If you get the grace thing, then church, however trying it might be, should not in any circumstances be making matters worse. Grace is simple counselling for the faith-stretched, for when it all seems too far-fetched, for when God seems distant.

Grace—absolutely amazing. You should do something but it doesn't matter if you do nothing. So have faith.

Pause for thought

Church, however trying it might be, should not in any circumstances be making matters worse.

Discussion questions

- **If you have come to life in Christ, what was it like before?**
- **How does it feel to have that previous life described as 'You were dead'?**

Prayer

Lord, help me to be grateful for that amazing gift of love, gracefully given by Jesus.

Part of the solution or part of the problem?

Now you are the body of Christ, and each one of you is a part of it.
1 CORINTHIANS 12:27

Our dependence on God, our love for him, and our desire to discover what he is up to and join him is the source of our action; it is our engine, our inspiration and our motivation.
STEVE CHALKE, *INTELLIGENT CHURCH* [30]

God uses us and our talents to build his kingdom. So a good vision for a church is to be the unique church that God wants us to be. Discerning the church's is not a one-person job. It will need hard work and prayer together. We must develop the skill of being able to spot what God is doing and go with it—which may mean abandoning our perfectly prepared plans.

A few years ago, by a twist of God-incidence, a large number of trained professional Christian youth workers ended up at the same church. I was one of them. I was stepping down from a role I had enjoyed at CYFA (the Church Youth Fellowships' Association) for the previous ten years and was working on the staff of a church as Associate Minister with responsibility for youth work. Alongside me was a trainee doing a placement while he carried on a degree in youth ministry, a youth pastor who had honed his skills with Careforce working with surfers in Cornwall, a curate who had been a youth worker before, and three or four volunteers with long experience of running summer camps and house parties. We looked at each other and thought, 'Either this is ridiculous over-provision or God wants to do amazing things among the young people here.'

Within a few months, without really trying, we became a student church. One Sunday early in the autumn term, a load of students who lived in town chose us. We had some hospitable families at the heart of things who were usually able to stretch their Sunday lunch to cover about 20 people without much notice. Word got about and, soon, up to 50 students were attending every Sunday morning.

We looked at each other again, wondering if anyone had any experience of working with students. None of us did. But we were a highly motivated, imaginative and adaptable bunch, and two of us moved out of work with teenagers to learn the skills of ministry to young adults.

I don't know how God's mind works. If I did, I would sell more books. But I have a hunch that he knew it would be safe to send some young adult Christians to our church because we wouldn't let them slip and we'd work out how to disciple them. And I believe we did.

Quoting an old businessman, Steve Chalke says, 'If it's neat, tidy, quiet and orderly that you're looking for, the graveyard is your only option.'[31]

I'll say it again: we must develop the skill of being able to spot what God is doing and go with it—which may mean abandoning our perfectly prepared plans.

Geographical inertia is a description of the state of affairs when an industry remains in a location long after the resource has been exhausted which was the reason for the original site. A glass manufacturer set up business in Nailsea, my home town, because there was a nearby source of energy—coal. The glass industry survived for a long time after the coal had run out.

Ecclesiastical inertia is a description of the state of affairs when an event continues to be constrained by circumstances that no longer apply. For example, an afternoon meeting finishes at 3.25p.m. so that members can pick up their children from school, even though the average age of the group is now 68 and most of their grandchildren have finished in education.

Whatever group or groups you belong to within a church, please be a critical friend. As a normal member of the church, the best gift you can give your leaders is to see things from the point of view of an outsider or stranger. Why do you still do a particular activity? Is it easy to find things out about it?

Here are some audit questions that anyone can ask about their group or meeting:

- Start time: was it fixed by a constraint that is no longer present? Would another time help people to join?
- What forces of inertia are exerting themselves in your church or meeting?
- Location: do you still meet in the best possible place? Do you imagine that you cannot move your church or meeting?
- Raw materials: what are they? Where are they?
- Names: are you called something that hides your true purpose or only makes sense to the people on the inside? Does your group do what it says on the tin?
- Purpose: have you done what you set out to do? Do you need to finish, or to do something else?

I was in the chapel of a retreat house, waiting for the noon Eucharist to begin. One of the four sisters in the chapel walked up to another, older nun and said, 'Do you have the chalice card?' Once discovered among the general debris of the pew shelf, a piece of pale blue, laminated card was handed over.

The first sister—a woman perhaps in her 40s, although the habit and head-covering may have aged her—walked across the chapel and placed it in front of a third nun, this one the oldest of the four by some distance. She tutted, then whispered, not quietly enough and to no one in particular, 'I did it yesterday.' She stood with some difficulty and shuffled ten feet to take the card to sister number four, who accepted it with resignation. She was now going to be the one to administer the Communion cup.

This act of supreme ordinariness, tetchiness and routine told more of the truth about community life than the Eucharist that followed. A great and noble attempt at poverty, chastity and obedience in this partly silent order had arrived at a state where notes were written on everything, from 'Not to be removed from the library' to 'Can any guest help with fruit picking this afternoon?'

This house where the order had renounced materialism was the most note-ridden, clutter-filled place I have ever been to. They may not have been writing their names on the eggs in the fridge, but pickiness was rife.

Human frailty, see. Can't live without it. What is the greatest attribute required of those who take on community life? Almost certainly forgiveness. I'd put money on it.

How do you get the hang of putting your faith to work? If you are a young Christian, I commend gap years. A number of organisations, such as *Time for God*, can help. One of the recent volunteers, at the end of the year, said this:

My year has been one of the most challenging but exciting times of my life. It has met every expectation I had, but in a different way to how I imagined, and added others. I have been stretched out of my comfort zone beyond belief but grown because of it in so many ways. I have made friends, gained a family and have learnt so much about God this year. If you want to learn more about God and strengthen your relationship with him, this is the gap year for you. It has also given me a flavour of church work, which I hope at some point God might call me back to.

And if you are not wanting to leave town for a gap year? Serve where you are—over and over and over.

I press on to take hold of that for which Christ Jesus took hold of me. (Philippians 3:12b)

There used to be the old comment that after the Lord Mayor's show, someone would have to go round the streets with a shovel. After the most exuberant and exciting events, you have to clear up.

For a couple of years I helped run three seven-day house parties in a row with a half-day off in between. You said goodbye to the members, quickly cleared up, took a break, then woke up the next morning to start again as if it was day one. The plan was that members arriving for Week 2 should be left with no idea that a previous house party had taken place. By the end of Week 2, the thought of 'going again' was not that enticing, but we did it.

After Week 3 we used to ask, 'Who is here to the bitter end?' In other words, who is not going home until the final clear-up is complete? The guy who trained me to run house parties used to say that the people you wanted on your team were the ones who trusted that somehow you would work out how to get them home after the clearing-up was finished, rather than worrying about it beforehand. Many of the people who made that sort of commitment are now involved in ministry themselves.

When we run our arts café project, we turn the Nailsea Trinity Centre into a funky lounge/bar for the night and then spend an hour recluttering it. We put back all the crèche toys, notices and ugly furniture we'd moved out to make the place nice. It's a bit depressing. I have noticed the members of the organising group who work their socks off, non-stop, so that we can get away by about midnight. Future ministers? Possibly.

Christian ministry is a series of events that need clearing up, and a long haul. The morning after the church council has made a commitment to a huge piece of new ministry—an exciting 'Yes'—the question hanging in the sky over all of us is, 'Will you go again?' To be honest, we've not put away the shovel after the previous exciting event. But of course we will—unanimously. It's service, see?

Here's an old joke.

A hot air balloon drifts slowly towards the ground and the guy in the gondola calls to a passer-by, 'Excuse me, but can you tell me where I am and how to get to the hot-air balloon convention?'

'Yes,' replies the man on the ground. 'You are at grid

square 3D on the local map page 43, you are floating ten metres above the ground, and, given your current position, I'd go by air.'

'Well thanks a bunch,' says the man in the balloon, 'Are you by any chance a management consultant?'

'I am,' he says. 'How did you know?'

'Well,' says the balloonist, 'everything you have told me is precise and true but none of it is the slightest use in getting where I want to get. You are a waste of time.'

'And tell me,' shouts the man on the ground to the balloon, now drifting off, 'are you a manager?'

'I am' says the balloonist. 'How did you know?'

'Let me see,' he says, 'you don't know where you are, you don't know where you are going, you haven't set out with instructions, you haven't the first idea how to phrase a question in order to improve matters, and you are in no worse a position than you were before you met me, yet somehow your predicament is now my fault.'

Well, I don't know if that would happen, but I do know that as we look at our vision for ourselves and for church and our part in it, we will need to be waiting on God, turning our dreams into action and focusing on the ultimate vision of Jesus coming again. But we need to know where we are.

The most important things that we need to remember about where we are can be found in Colossians 3. It begins, 'Since, then, you have been raised with Christ...' (v. 1a). Those words tell us the first thing: we are Christ's people. 'Jesus-people' may not be a comfortable label to wear, but it's there. We have our hearts above. We are the people in our city, town or village who think differently.

Colossians 3 continues, 'Set your hearts on things above,

where Christ is seated at the right hand of God... When Christ, who is your life, appears, then you also will appear with him in glory' (vv. 1b, 4).

As Christians, with our hearts set above, we are people of a different destiny. So while we should feel an urgency about having others to join us on our journey, our destination is not in any doubt. We know what's written on the last page. We are future people. 'Do not rejoice that the spirits submit to you, but rejoice that your names are written in heaven' (Luke 10:20). Jesus said this to the 72 disciples he had sent out two by two.

'Put to death therefore, whatever belongs to the earthly nature... [and] put on the new self' (Colossians 3:5a, 10a). We start out as different people. Our behaviour and relationships are those of people who have different attitudes from the rest of the population. Of course, goodness, mercy, sacrifice and generosity are not things you find only in Christians, but Colossians suggests that we should take a lead.

There's more: 'Here there is no Greek or Jew, circumcised or uncircumcised, barbarian, Scythian, slave or free, but Christ is all, and is in all' (v. 11). The same thought is found in Galatians 3:28. We should be inclusive people. We take very seriously any charge of prejudice or exclusivity. Our churches should be representative of our communities. If they are not, we are doing something wrong.

On top of this: 'Bear with each other and forgive whatever grievances you may have against one another. Forgive as the Lord forgave you' (v. 13). We are loving people. We do to others what we'd want them to do to us. And if things go wrong, we forgive, quickly. We hold no grudges.

We are also congregational people. We gather together. If we don't join the gathering, we are missed. All this advice to the Colossian Christians was in the context and with the expectation that they were part of a church that met together. How can you develop grudges and poor relationships that need to be corrected and forgiven if you don't meet?

- Jesus people
- Future people
- Different people
- Inclusive people
- Loving people
- Congregational people

If that was the distinctive pattern set by Paul writing to a bunch of Christians about 2000 years ago, who are we now? I think we are good at being many of those things, but we have also become:

- Shrinking people. Attendance at churches has fallen away.
- Inward-looking people. We can be preoccupied with keeping our church show on the road: 'more about maintenance than mission' is the jargon of the day. Try to spend as much time as possible in relationship with people who do not know Jesus. It is important.
- 'Now' people. We are very preoccupied with the affairs of now and have not lifted our eyes much over the last few years to look at where we are going.

The writer Douglas Adams said that society's development has brought a change to the great questions of life. To paraphrase, what started out as 'When will we eat?' became 'What will we eat?' and is now 'Where shall we eat?'

The 'when' of the church is the future and Jesus' return. The 'what' of the church has been much discussed, perhaps even overdiscussed. So 'Where is this church going?' is the question to move on to. There are so many things we could do. Where shall we go? Where shall we eat?

I am not so naive as to think that any of this will happen in our own strength. If, for some reason, God does not want to move a church on, it will stay stuck. But I am determined not to be the obstacle, if I can avoid it, to God's work. You too?

As we've been looking at some of Paul's teaching on church in the New Testament, we've also been dipping into some of the letters to the churches in the book of Revelation. Our final visit is coming up—to Pergamum.

Pergamum was in the Roman province of Asia (it's in Turkey today) and a key city in that province, although Ephesus was the commercial centre. It had a fantastic library and our word 'parchment' is derived from the city's name.

The city had worshipped the Emperor—for whom the symbol might well be a sharp, double-edged, Roman sword. But it is not the Emperor who holds the sword here. It is the speaker of the prophetic words of judgment. It is God: 'These are the words of him who has the sharp, double-edged sword' (Revelation 2:12). He has a sword.

Pergamum has been a tough place in which to witness to Jesus and there have been casualties, but some have stood firm and been faithful: 'You did not renounce your faith in me, even in the days of Antipas, my faithful witness, who was put to death in your city' (v. 13b).

So what's the problem at Pergamum? Well, not a clever one, frankly. It is not a comfortable place for an angel to be living:' '… where Satan has his throne' (v. 13a). There have been problems in the church there—problems of error, problems of compromise, and a problem that was so obvious to the writer that it wasn't spelled out.

One of the difficulties of witnessing to the gospel today is that people have a portfolio approach to life.

'Have some Jesus.'

'Thanks, I'll add that to what I already believe.'

Even if this creates paradoxes, people will not be entirely uncomfortable with it. Relativism—the idea that you believe what's good for you and I believe what's good for me, that beliefs are all relative—has caused us some problems. People don't like the idea of Jesus clearing out all their other beliefs. They would like Christ-plus. They would like to compromise. But compromising means accepting part-error. If I compromise with you, I give a bit and you give a bit: both of us lose something.

If you have decided to live as a Christian and be part of a Christian community, you need to allow Jesus to influence everything else. He is like a bright light shining into the dark recesses of our lives. If there's some dirt there, it will need cleaning up. If there is some aspect of my life that I keep hidden out of sight, where Jesus is not allowed in, I am simply not living as a Christian.

For Pergamum, the place with the good library, the writing was on the wall—unless they repented, in which case the writing was to be fresh and clean: a guarantee of future security in Christ, and a little secret: 'To him who overcomes, I will give… a white stone with a new name written on it, known only to him who receives it' (v. 17b).

A new name, on a white stone. The idea of God having a relationship with you, with me, which leads to him calling me something that no one else calls me, is quite an intimate thought.

This is the future for those who repent. It always is. Repent of what? You probably know.

Pause for thought

'God's endless improvisatory technique means that he can bestow gifts on the church in its current breadth even though its current breadth was not his original idea.'
(ARCHBISHOP ROWAN WILLIAMS, PUBLIC LECTURE, 2010)

Discussion questions

- Is there ever a time when it is appropriate for a non-leader to be moving on to a different church? In what circumstances?
- Are you playing your part, finding your gifts, serving God all your days? If not, what needs to happen to change the situation?

Prayer

Lord, write my new name on a white stone.

— ❖ —

Conclusion

I mentioned that I would tell you what happened when Trendlewood Church moved schools. We moved. Our first Sunday was good and got a lot of splash in the press. Our Bishop came. Visitors came. The next Sunday was Easter Sunday, and we had a good congregation and a lively all-age celebration (after a brief panic when we were locked out and had to wake a caretaker).

We have been there a month now and have, I fear, got back to normal. This normal may be a new normal, but it is normal. Comfortable. OK. I don't want to be that sort of normal .

Our church will not grow just because we changed venue. We need to get out and meet our new neighbours, improve our publicity, invite guests to our social events. And I mean, 'We'.

I have struggled all my life, guiltily, as most Christians have, with the idea that I am not praying enough. Christians are not a difficult bunch in whom to engender guilt. All you have to do is cast doubt on the quality or quantity of someone's prayer life and they will admit failure in an instant.

Until recently I would have done so myself. Then I got it. I didn't run around town naked, you'll be glad to know, but it was a 'Eureka!' moment (deserving of the only exclamation mark I've used in this book).

I've put a prayer at the end of each chapter, but I've concluded that the only prayer really worth praying is, 'Lord,

I'm listening.' If you hear the voice of God, through his word, through other people or through circumstances, fancy even beginning to imagine that he would call you and not equip you until you asked him to. It would be like an army officer seeing his battered and bloodied men return from the front, and saying, 'I wondered when you were going to ask me for weapons; they're over there.'

If God wants you to do something, you'll know. You'll hear him asking. Then he'll equip you.

I am praying enough. I have a vision of the best church for miles and miles. I know, I know, I've said that. But I do. So I'm waiting, hoping, trusting.

A few years ago, I heard that a newspaper ran a competition for the best letter on the subject 'What is wrong with the world?'

I also heard that the prize was won by the shortest letter they received. It went:

Dear Sir,
I am.
Yours faithfully

Changing your church involves changing you. Sorry. If this book has started you on that journey, then I am delighted and also sorry that I've introduced you to hardship.

There would be no point in producing a feedback form. It would be like punching you in the face and asking for your observations on the quality of the blow.

Being a normal member of the church involves being a normal Christian. And normal Christians will stand out because, in the eyes of the rest of the world, we will be weird. Outstanding, but odd. Try it.

Feedback is welcome on Twitter @s1eve, via stevetilley.blogspot.com or any other way you can think of. I could hardly not say that after what I've written earlier.

Thank you for reading.

Notes

1 Stephen Cottrell, Bishop of Chelmsford, at the Church of England's National Stewardship Advisers' Conference, Hothorpe Hall, January 2002.
2 Brian McLaren, *A New Kind of Christian* (Jossey-Bass, 2001).
3 Peter Carey, *Illywhacker* (University of Queensland Press, 1985).
4 Douglas Coupland, *Player One* (Heinemann, 2010).
5 Pauline, stevetilley.blogspot.com, 3/11.
6 Mitch Albon, *Have a Little Faith* (Sphere, 2009).
7 www.alabama3.co.uk/en/general_articles/about
8 Alec Motyer, *The Message of Philippians*, BST Series (IVP, 1984).
9 David Watson (heard in a taped talk in the 1980s).
10 Nick Hornby, *How To Be Good* (Penguin, 2001).
11 Steve Tilley, *Mustard Seed Shavings* (BRF, 2011).
12 Francis Foulkes, *Ephesians* (IVP, 1956).
13 Philip Pullman, *Start the Week* (Radio 4, 5/4/10).
14 Michael Wilcock, *The Message of Revelation*, BST Series, (IVP, 1975).
15 Eddie Gibbs (ed.), *Ten Growing Churches* (MARC Europe, 1984).
16 Tom Peters, *Thriving on Chaos* (Harper Perennial, 1987).
17 Eagle Star Birmingham, 1974.
18 Philip Pullman, *The Good Man Jesus and the Scoundrel Christ* (Canongate, 2010).
19 John Wimber, *Christian World News Review* (October 1993).
20 George Herbert, 'Teach me, my God and King' (1633).
21 Joy Press, *The Killing of Crusty* (*Spin* Magazine 1994, quoted in the *Faber Book of Pop*).
22 Michael Cole, *He Is Lord* (Hodder and Stoughton, 1987).
23 Mark Greene, *The Great Divide* (LICC, 2010).
24 Quoted by Brian McLaren in *A New Kind of Christianity*.
25 David Prior, *The Message of 1 Corinthians* (IVP/BST, 1985).
26 Bishop Peter Price at an induction service, 2010

27 Antony Billington with Margaret Killingray and Helen Parry, *Whole Life, Whole Bible* (BRF, 2012), p. 143.
28 Christopher Idle, *Hope for the Church of England* (ed. Gavin Reid), (Kingsway, 1986).
29 Gordon Jones, *The Church Without Walls* (Marshalls, 1985).
30 Steve Chalke, *Intelligent Church* (Zondervan, 2006).
31 Chalke, *Intelligent Church*.

Also by Steve Tilley

Mustard Seed Shavings

Mountain-moving for beginners

Taken a first step of faith—or a first step in taking faith more seriously—but don't quite know what to do next? Possibly this book will be useful.

Mustard Seed Shavings offers a gentle introduction to Christian lifestyle, using the Ten Commandments as a framework. It tries to show what following Jesus means in practice today. Hopefully it reads more like receiving a present than being given a rule-book.

Each chapter ends with a pause for thought, a couple of discussion questions and a brief prayer. So, not the last word or the tiny details, but perhaps a nice place to begin.

ISBN 978 1 84101 828 7   £6.99
Available from your local Christian bookshop or direct from BRF: visit www.brfonline.org.uk

Also from BRF

Come and See

Learning from the life of Peter

Stephen Cottrell

When we look at the life of Peter—fisherman, disciple, leader of the Church—we find somebody who responded wholeheartedly to the call to 'come and see'. Come and meet Jesus, come and follow him, come and find your life being transformed. This book focuses on Peter, not because he is the best-known of Jesus' friends, nor the most loyal, but because he shows us what being a disciple of Jesus is actually like. Like us, he takes a step of faith and then flounders, and needs the saving touch of God to continue becoming the person he was created to be.

Come and See is also designed to help you begin to develop a pattern of Bible reading, reflection and prayer. Twenty-eight readings, arranged in four sections, offer short passages from the story of Peter, plus comment and questions for personal response or group discussion.

ISBN 978 1 84101 843 0   £6.99
Available from your local Christian bookshop or direct from BRF: visit www.brfonline.org.uk

Also from BRF

Whole Life, Whole Bible

50 readings on living in the light of Scripture

Antony Billington
with Margaret Killingray and Helen Parry

Where we spend most of our time—at home, at work, in the neighbourhood—matters to God and to his mission in and for the world. Far from restricting our faith to the 'personal' sphere, disengaged from everyday living, Scripture encourages us to take the Lord of life into the whole of life.

Whole Life, Whole Bible is written from the conviction that God's word illuminates every part of existence, enabling us to see differently and live differently—from Monday to Sunday, in public as well as in private. A walk through the unfolding story of the Bible in 50 readings and reflections shows how our lives are bound up with, and shaped by, God's plan to restore a broken universe. That big story forms our minds, fuels our imaginations and fashions our daily life as we live in God's world, in the light of God's word, wherever we are.

ISBN 978 0 85746 017 2   £6.99
Available from your local Christian bookshop or direct from BRF: visit www.brfonline.org.uk

Also available for Kindle

Also from BRF

One Dad Encountering God

Brad Lincoln

What if God has left an important clue about his personality somewhere inside us, as if, in making us, he left his signature?

This book shares the reflections of one ordinary man about what it means to be a dad—and how that fits in with his feelings about life, the universe and God. If we are made in the image of our heavenly Father, we can learn a lot about what it means to be a dad through looking at what God is like. And reflecting on our relationship with our own children can help us begin to glimpse how God feels about us. *One Dad Encountering God* does not set out to provide all the answers but to get you thinking about what really matters in life.

ISBN 978 1 84101 678 8   £6.99
Available from your local Christian bookshop or direct from BRF: visit www.brfonline.org.uk

Enjoyed this book?

Write a review—we'd love to hear what you think.
Email: reviews@brf.org.uk

Keep up to date—receive details of our new books as they happen.
Sign up for email news and select your interest groups at:
www.brfonline.org.uk/findoutmore/

Follow us on Twitter @brfonline

By post—to receive new title information by post (UK only), complete the form below and post to: BRF Mailing Lists, 15 The Chambers, Vineyard, Abingdon, Oxfordshire, OX14 3FE

Your Details
Name _____
Address _____
_____
Town/City _____ Post Code _____
Email _____

Your Interest Groups (*Please tick as appropriate)	
❏ Advent/Lent	❏ Messy Church
❏ Bible Reading & Study	❏ Pastoral
❏ Children's Books	❏ Prayer & Spirituality
❏ Discipleship	❏ Resources for Children's Church
❏ Leadership	❏ Resources for Schools

Support your local bookshop
Ask about their new title information schemes.